WISDOM WISDOM

WISDOM WISDOM

WISDOM WISDOM

WISDOM WISDOM

WISDOM WISDOM

1-800-OLD-PEOPLE-MATTER

contemporary writs by

CHRIS BENT

www.chrisbent.com

Published in the USA by Chris Bent
Naples, Florida USA
http://ChrisBent.com

1-800-I-AM-UNHAPPY,
1-800-FOR-WOMEN-ONLY,
1-800-LAUGHING-OUT-LOUD,
1-800-OH-MY-GOODNESS,
1-800-FOR-SEALS-ONLY
1-800-OH-MY-DONALD
1-800-FOR-VETERANS-ONLY
1-800-ONLY-FOR-LOVE, and
1-800-OH-MY-BLACKNESS
are trademarks owned by
Chris Bent and are used with his permission.

————◆•◆•◆————

Also By Chris Bent

Available in Paperback and Electronic Versions

1-800-I-AM-UNHAPPY
Volume 1

1-800-I-AM-UNHAPPY
Volume 2

1-800-FOR-WOMEN-ONLY

1-800-LAUGHING-OUT-LOUD

1-800-OH-MY-GOODNESS

1-800-FOR-SEALS-ONLY

1-800-OH-MY-DONALD

1-800-FOR-VETERANS-ONLY

1-800-ONLY-FOR-LOVE

1-800-OH-MY-BLACKNESS

Praise for
1-800-Old-People-Matter

"Despite the title, this book provides wisdom for all ages with the key message that a person's true beauty, strength, and age lies within. Worth a read."

Michael Hopkins, Attorney at Law, Naples, FL

There's a lot of wisdom within these pages. And, sad to say, who better to judge than us "old people."

Dr. Francis B. Cleary (Retired)
Senior Dental Staff and OPD Director, Hartford Hospital, Hartford, CT

Chris Bent has a real gift for writing thought provoking books with short chapters....each of which has humor, a catchy literary style, and a powerful message on which to reflect. Chris's overriding message is to live the Golden Rule, reaching out to assist others while also looking inward to address our own shortcomings. Collectively, his thoughts convey a clarion call for all of us to look beyond self-satisfaction and to focus on what we can do to help others and to better the world in which we live. Presented without espousing specific religious doctrine, his latest book is a page turner--always encouraging the reader to see what is next in Chris's captivating messages.

John E. Sampson, Retired Fortune 500 Senior Executive

Here's the "how to" when approaching Chris' writing: Read one a day, because it takes 24 hours to glean the depth of the message. Having now told you the "how to", let me expand on the why.

Some of his writings make me smile or laugh out loud. Others make me very pensive and contemplative. Oh, but there's more: I often agree with his philosophy yet other times I spend the remaining hours mentally arguing that he's wrong.

So, what does this prove? It proves that he's a "good read". Keep the mental games going Chris.

From an old woman who calls you Friend.

Nancy Lascheid, RN, BSN, Co-Founder
Neighborhood Health Clinic, Naples, Florida

More reviews of Chris Bent's books can be found in the
"In The Words Of Others" section at the back of this book.

To Christina, Candice, Courtney and their journeys, and to all the young people who won't listen to the old people.

Prologue

This book is meant to bring us closer to recapturing our youth through sharing our wisdom. If one chapter touches one person then it was not in vain. You may laugh or cry or shake your fist. But you are not done if you read between the lines. Old People Matter more than ever.

Chris Bent

Naples
January 2017
www.ChrisBent.com

Contents

Chapters

Forever Young

Forever Young!! Screams every ad on TV, magazines, cell phone, computer.

You cannot escape the promises inferred.

Bye-bye wrinkles, old teeth, paunch, and innumerable imperfections and conditions.

Try and look at anything on your iPad and you have to work around the Forever Young ads which have all these hidden buttons. Obscuring the truth. NIGHTMARE!!

Why does Forever Young rate so high amongst all the scams. Want to see its ultimate aberration. Look 15 seconds at "Housewives of Southern Idaho"… LOL

Under the pretense that this is the look for all housewives to aspire to. "Housewives of Plasticville". Look at cosmetic ads which cost fortunes for the right model and photograph… as if it were normal…?? How many jars can one buy…?? That overfill hidden drawers?? Not to say that men don't look in the mirror too…

You want to stay young? Want to have that seductive "assurance" twinkle in your eyes after 80?

Bye-Bye Wrinkles.

All you have to do is know something that others don't. The curious will want to know why, but will be afraid to ask. For inside, you can feel young if you know you have meaning. If you know you are helping someone else. That you are important to someone else. It's more than advice. It's showing love by being honest and caring.

Nothing gives you a better shot of pride than that. "Lovetox", the new injection for your lips and eyes. Only creates a glow… not something that does not move.

What you eat, what you touch, what you say…. If it is from the love and truth spot deep within… others will only see you as forever young.

They won't give a damn about your wrinkles or grey hair.

They will want to be close, to be next to your "Forever Young" heart.

And you will be laughing with them.

Ageless……..

Celebrity

Why are celebrities so lucky?

Because they get so much money?

Because people want them at their party?

A "selfie" with a celebrity is the ultimate experience of the times. Celebrities can wear whatever they want and be cool…. But beneath most of the torn jeans are distressed hearts. Not knowing if they have really earned praise for superficial efforts. Insecurities plague them. Masterfully hidden until they trip into the scandal sheets. Exciting parties, eyes glancing, moments fulfilled, in empty rooms.

It's funny that we all start as a celebrity with our first breath!

Smiling faces, coochie coo to me and you…

Infants clothes, kids clothes, teen clothes, wedding clothes… all celebrity clothes. Even the Uniform makes one a celebrity. Always to someone… celebrities are false heroes. Real heroes put their lives on the line for good. If you call them a hero or a celebrity, they just look down. A Jimmy Stewart "aw shucks" is the sign of a real celebrity.

Why are celebrities so lucky?

You have to be really bad not to be a celebrity to someone. But then again if you're really bad, you become an infamous celebrity. Intelligent choice.

Old people are my celebrities. They know so much more and they listen as if you matter… if what you are saying matters… Respect and manners count. Making them feel important opens unimaginable doors. It means you have to give to get. Humility and sharing some of your journey is essential. Smiles will form as you become a celebrity to one another. Unavoidable.

With children you already are a celebrity. They are dying to know something about you. They need truth. Whatever we say must be "true". Someday they will remember that "true" you told them and it will help them. Old people can be the foundation of Truth for young and old.

To tell you the truth, the truth matters… Just Sayin'.

Truth is the spotlight that makes us a celebrity.

Take a bow….

PTSD

Thanks.

From all of us.

Courage is a poem.

A poem of life for others.

Mud is dirty and hard to walk in.

Like life, one must go places to get to the Place.

Where one can feel proud and good again.

The greater the test, the greater the victory.

Be it against the enemy or the self.

Get dirty America.

Save yourself.

Listen to the once lost.

Zero to 60

Car magazines were the escape for the male 50 years ago...

In fact, in the 1950's under 10 seconds was special.

Beating another car by even 1/10th of a second was a marketing windfall to young and old eyes alike.

The record today is 2.2 seconds by the Porsche 918 Spyder. Whew... dream territory....

How did we get so fast so fast?? It is 2016 and it was 66 years ago that I was 10. Been watching lapsed times for that long...

A lot happens to everyone in that amount of time. Good things and bad things. Pain and joy. All unexpected. In fact, everything is unexpected. When you are young you feel so good that your expectations are muted by exuberance and health.

Fast cars don't mean you will get there sooner. In fact, living life fast means you don't get to see as much. Pretending you are something you are not yet means no growth. The fast lane is for fools. Only when you are much older do you understand that.

Growth and happiness...?? At what speed?? How to get to where you want to go. Like Olympians, training and training and

repeating and repeating makes you good at your specialty. At your job or with your family doing the same thing well over and over builds strength and satisfaction.

Now the road we choose becomes critical. Good pavement or bad pavement? Smooth or rough. It is our choice. Except that it takes time to be good, to be kind, to be compassionate, to know truth, and to show that you love others more than yourself. That is the easy road if you find it.

Old people know.

Life forgives if you learn from mistakes.

Life forgives if you learn to forgive.

Most old people don't talk much about their real journey. They are dying to if you ever knew the right questions to ask in the right way. It will be spellbinding and their precious gift to you.

Zero to 60 is no longer meaningful to me.

I am 16 years beyond that.

Burned some rubber......

Senior Moment

Wait a moment….

There is something important…

To tell you.

Wait!!!

Darn it…

What did I last say?

Maybe we can label them "Fleeting Moments"? Moments that got away.

There are so many moments in life. Some filled with laughter. Some filled with pain. Some filled with regret. Some filled with hope. Moments are specific places in time.

We wish that many did not happen. But they did. And maybe still do if they haunt our inner being. They can go away but we will need a moment to figure it out. Maybe a moment to forgive.

Now we seniors have to watch our steps and our health. There are two things I am always looking out for… not falling… and the next chair. Mental alertness is no longer a given. LOL.

Now we seniors have to watch our steps.

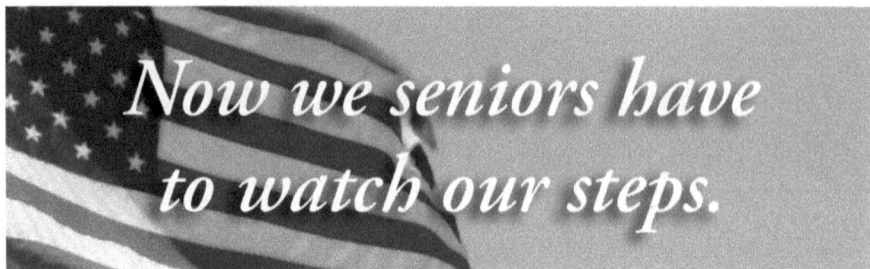

Any moment lapsed can have serious complications. That is why you see a lot of us talking to ourselves.

"Hey gramps…. what are you thinking about?"

Often the question cannot be answered as you were avoiding thinking…. But this is the most special of all moments…when your grandchild askes you a question. It must be seized with truth and love. Gramp's inner being must be passed on. A seed of integrity and compassion must be planted. Our gift to our bloodline and this moment and this child.

Wisdom comes with age.
Every effort must be made to pass it on.
Otherwise we might as well have never existed.
So Seniors, seize the moment.
Make it a legacy moment.
And smile within.

Beatles

Can you remember the moment when THEY stepped off the plane?

We were young. TV was black and white. Values were pretty much too....

The good old days.

Girls were screaming and fainting. The Beatles' crazy haircuts and music overwhelmed the next years. Everything Beatles. Instant freedom. New subcultures formed. Their music was almost social networking without the electronics.

They wrote 300 songs....every one over the years helped us retain our youth. Amazing. And did they tackle Love.... Read a title and the melody still plays in our grey hair world.... "All You Need Is Love, And I Love Her, Help, Can't Buy Me Love, I Want To Hold Your Hand, Love Me Do, She Loves You, Yesterday".

Old people know this better than young people because we were there... and the music still keeps us young. Still popping up... We still get to smile.

The black and white decade of the 50's was, looking back,

Girls were screaming and fainting.

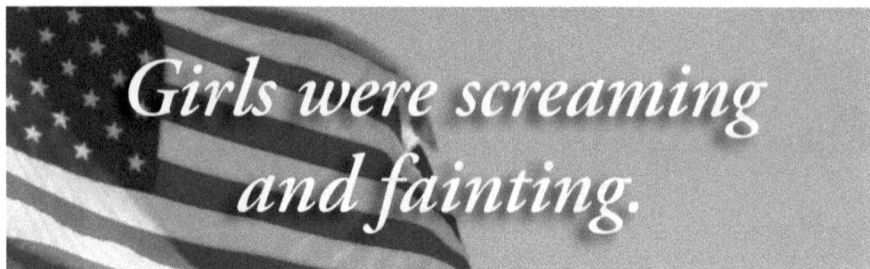

fabulous…. Edward R. Murrow, Lawrence Welk, What's My Line, Eric Sevareid, Johnny Carson, I love Lucy, Roy Rogers, Flash Gordon, and for me, Sea Hunt. Don't all these names make us smile?? Good days. Walk home from school, no worries.

There were wonderful radio shows. I built my own crystal set. I remember scratching the crystal with a pin and getting a station. Wow! Radio consoles became big pieces of furniture.

I loved "Suspense, Dragnet, Lone Ranger, Jack Benny, X Minus One, Lights Out…." These were this boy's shows… Love to hear from you girls what your favorites were……

Then television took over and we now have 50" Curved Samsung screens with perfect color and too many commercials making life ageless. Or making us age…as we quickly change channels during commercials…

And do you believe all the smiley spots aimed right at us??? Reverse mortgage, skin remedies (ha), potency gambles.

Young people today know too much about too much.

Social networking makes everything believable.

War is looming.

We pretend evil is only in the movies.

Land again Beatles.

We loved Love.

Old Girls Matter

I sent this old girl, who happens to be a friend, not a girlfriend, the previous chapter just written yesterday… BEATLES…

Her name is Nancy. She has built a health clinic that serves those who don't fit into the system, that fall through the cracks, who can't afford health care. Dozens of doctors and nurses volunteer on the side… amazing. Selfless love.

Anyway, she shot back a positive comment…whew… and then went on to say, "What about girls?" I didn't realize I was not inclusive…LOL.

"Saddle shoes, bobby socks, poodle skirts (below the knees), high neck long sleeve sweaters and pearls". Huuuh? "Is she from Mars?" a teenager of today would say. Google doesn't cover Mars… maybe Siri does…

"Homework done at the kitchen table with paper and pen". I don't think that is girls only…

"Slow dancing, girls on one side of the gymnasium and the boys on the other". This explains why I was afraid of girls. Sitting on the opposite side with nervousness, new and scary. Having to

Her name is Nancy.

slowly, properly, walk across and get your card filled… I'd rather parachute out of a helicopter.

"Going steady and fraternity pins". Is this what girls dreamed of? A guy to go steady with who was wearing a fraternity pin? Good luck… and maybe bad choice. Oops I got one in college…

"Hours on the land line phone". Ok…Stupid… gossip university at too young an age. We had sports and sports and sports….

"Who's turn to wash or dry the dinner dishes?" Okay… now that sounds right. Girls gotta be pros in the kitchen. Guys have sports, camping, mowing the lawn, and beer.

"Family vacations"… maybe the most important of all as we had to live together away from home. You had to look out for your brother or sister…. And parents could control the rules of fun and love… they were great.

Many kids never get vacations together as parents have split or gone. Tough subject.

"Curfews". A relic of the past and never needed more than today. Parental control has been subordinated to the emotions of the child be they 12 or 20… if… they ever look up from the cellphone...

Lastly Nancy said "Respect for others". That's all I preach and pray for. That it makes a return and restores our dignity.

We need The Beatles to land again.

All we need is Love...

One Pant Leg

OPL stands for so many things.

Of course you think it is Old People...something.

Like Old People Listen?... and Old People Love?....

Well you are wrong.

In the private world of the aging there are thoughts and unspoken concerns as the body changes. Women are even more fearful of the mirror, and men that their physical skills are fading. Men pursue their sports hoping to replicate some greatness...but they realize they can't throw as far or dunk anything.

Much of the conversations are given to times lost and feats remembered. The physical world is no longer the same. For some there are new medical conditions that turns lives upside down. More change than had been expected. Then there are relationships fading and problems within the greater family.

You know so much more, but the young are too busy to listen. You never hear "grandpa, what should I do about this problem?" And you could have the answer...

So it is time to laugh.

Of course, I never said "Dad, I need some advice…"

So how do we know when we are old?

Probably when we are so involved in maintaining our well-being.

However, I now know that well-being means how much "well" you bring to another.

Helping others is the only thing that can keep one young. It really, really does. You don't care what others think. You just feel young and "good" when you help others laugh or share their tears or serve them in some very small way.

So it is time to laugh. I want to be compassionate and at the same time help others smile. So here is what OPL means. One Pant Leg. And it sure told me I was finally old.

I was in the local Wellness Center, don't you love that name?… The average age is way up there except for the muscled mirror addicts. I had done my machines and my 110 lb. abdomen crunch… (which reduces all bellies). I was putting on my shorts and finally succeeded in putting both legs into one leg hole of my shorts. For a moment feeling like an idiot, then inconspicuously moving my right leg into the other pant hole.

I had graduated into geezerdom.

I am officially an old man.

One Pant Leg at a time.

Musical Chairs 1

Come on…. Tell me you remember this game. Musical Chairs.

It is being played internationally. Dead serious.

In the Middle East certain countries are trying to sit in chairs occupied.

It is called Musical Misery.

Genocide is what happens when people are not allowed to sit in their chair. The chair they have owned for centuries. Go figure?

The term "musical chairs" is used in Washington. Who knows who is going to run what next?

How are we going to survive if there is always one chair missing?

The game is so much fun to play with your family at a picnic or in a home when the fire is on and the snow is falling. Maybe down in a rec room. A dozen chairs are put in a circle. 13 people circle as music is played. It then is stopped suddenly and everybody scrambles to a chair. One person, in deep sadness, does not find one…or cannot out fight the possessor. He is eliminated. One

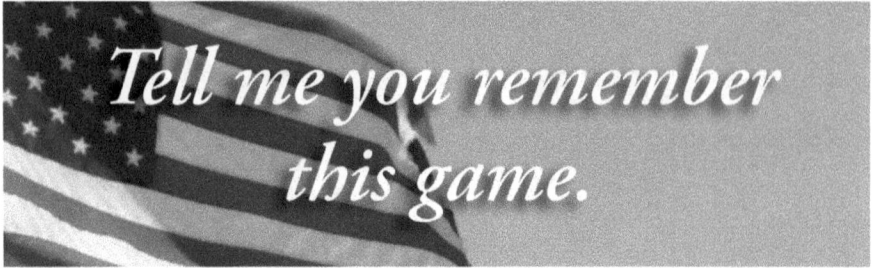

more chair is removed. There are now 11 chairs for 12 people or…kids. Fun. Good old fashioned fun.

Now this old person has a different take on it now. Wherever I go (am taken) I have to be alert for the next chair. I don't like standing like I used to. Often I get to stay in the car in a Home Goods parking lot. I know tons of them. Hey, I have my iPad and iPhone so can remain relevant or entertained.

I am always looking for the next chair. Except there are usually other old people doing the same. The "Dance of the Elderlies". Store music doesn't help as it is usually awful. Sometimes just leaning on the shopping cart in a large store is all you get.

Eyes still intensely looking for an empty chair. In the furniture part or certainly at checkout. Shopping…. Don't get me started.

Real estate prices go up when demand exceeds supply.

Musical chairs.

Musical Chairs 2

Come on…. Tell me you remember this game. Musical Chairs 2?

It is being played internationally.

Dead serious.

Shame on them.

In America it's a little better….

"The Magical Mystery Tour is waiting to take you away". No… Call it The Musical Mystery Chairs Tour. It is played out every day in every home.

All our lives we do our best to insure there is a chair for everyone at Thanksgiving Dinner. Calls are made and remade to insure little Carlos is coming…hopefully no longer suffering from a cold. And will Hilda be able to make it after having a really tough time last night with her boyfriend? You get the musical picture?

Thanksgiving is such a fun time if you have a large enough table. So nobody has to eat on a tray in the other room. Thanksgiving is a time to reflect on being blessed to sit at a table and have turkey and wine when half the world is starving.

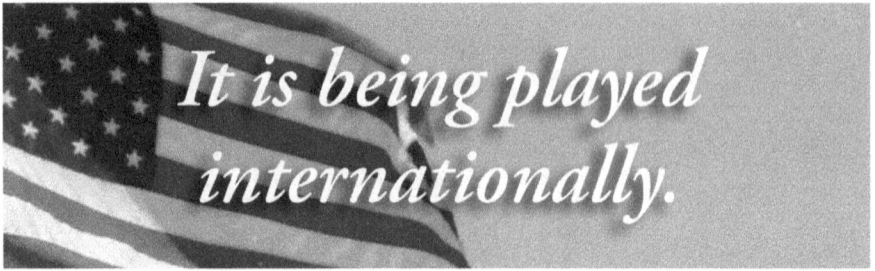

It is being played internationally.

I have a new concept for the game! When there is no chair for you at the table you have to go out and buy a meal for someone in need. The needy hide; they are embarrassed. Might take a little bit of effort to find them... but the reward is 10 fold.

You will have created a chair at a table for someone who has no table much less a chair.

You may have lost musical chairs but you have created a seat of pride within.

You will know it and the person you gave the chair to will too.

It's kinda like a Lone Ranger kind of thing.

"Hi Ho Silver"... riding off and not looking back.

You can play Musical Mystery Chairs every day.

It's Magic.

The Fall

It's just orange.

A rust color.

The way it should be.

The leaves will soon fall but not before they reach their autumn majesty. People from all over the world travel to New England to see this symphony of leaves before they fall.

Is that they "fall" the reason for the name? After all its glory, beauty falls to the ground, decomposes, and becomes fertilizer for a future Fall.

Of course there is our Niagara Falls where nothing changes. The constant roar of life's fuel moving on…. I wonder how long it has been doing that? And where the water really comes from? Just think… No water No life. And no more bottled water to carry around like jewelry. Life does have its humor….

Now if a woman wants to be really attractive she buys a fall. And becomes almost like a lioness with her mane… LOL

Now to get serious we geezers are always looking out for the next

The leaves will soon fall.

thing to trip over. Hip replacement is not fun. We hear the stories of others falling and breaking bones.

Recovery is slow with old bones.

The worst part is the sense of stupidity for something which could have been avoided. And then you depend on others to help you until healed. This is where true friends come forth. Genuine concern is treasured gift.

Everyone falls in a different place at an unexpected time. It would be great to have some statistics on locations... a store, a gas station, a restaurant, the dining room, the living room, the staircase, and on and on.

Love those motorized staircase chairs.

Our minds tend to wander as we age. Our concentration and focus starts to get impaired. No longer having a job to go to has its challenges. What is off in 'the not so far away" distance is "The End."... If.... you don't believe....

Our reality is today and it is so real that we never really think of the future. There are wounds to reconcile.

Acts that make a difference are important.

The only way to make one feel young.

Let me help just one more person .... I pray....

Oops... I just missed the last step....

Wrinkle Power

When we see wrinkles grow over the years we think it means a loss of power, of being less of that which matters.

It is tough to stand in the front of your mirror in the morning. Brushing your teeth and checking their whiteness. In some kind of dance of vanity.

What to wear becomes more difficult for the woman as she reluctantly shoulders her "wrinklephobia". Makeup and hair are even more important.... Until they are not.

It's not the face stupid, it's the heart. There are no wrinkles on hearts as far as I can see. Maybe a stent or bypass will allow one to live longer and collect more wrinkles?

But that is not a desired outcome... having a working heart longer allows you to do things that matter a little longer. Until…??....

With age one learns what life is and what it is not. Young people do not have that wisdom. They gotta get old before the light goes on. We can mean so much to others with our wisdom. We often sell our importance short.

Power to the Wrinkled.

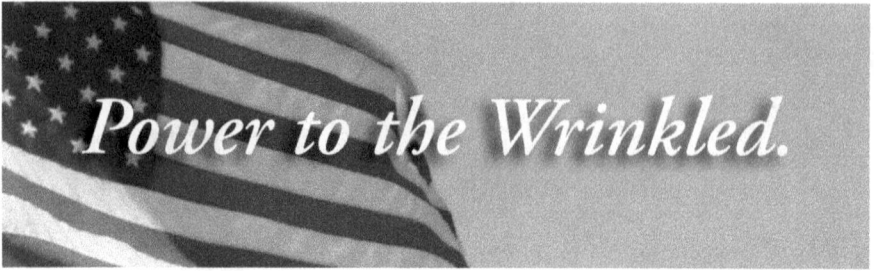

There is wrinkle power that smooth skin doesn't have. Kids can look up to wrinkles as it is the sign of those who know and can help...with courage.

Wrinkle power is accepting yourself fully for what you are. Then getting off your old wrinkled "arse" and looking for people to help... in the smallest of ways. All of a sudden you will feel a new vigor and relevance. You will look in the mirror and be proud of what you see and the wrinkles will not be seen nor matter.

Power to the Wrinkled.

Let's take our country and world back with values and determination. We have seen evil. We know it deserves nothing.

Speak out all "wrinkled"...

We need to take mankind back from its fatally erred path.

Wrinkled fists into the air!

Thy will be done.

Recyclable Plastic

When HDPE (High-Density Polyethylene) plastic is finished being used it is tossed away and often found floating in the oceans and rivers.

After what was inside is consumed it no longer has any value.

The outside of the product is abandoned… except when recycled at redemption centers.

Hmm… a little interesting…don't you think??

In 3 generations the use of plastic has exploded. It serves and it destroys when abandoned. Ever see a bottle stuck in a pelican's throat… much less in the stomachs of fish and animals. Plastic debris is on our ocean floors and going everywhere on the surfaces. Waves go up and down with hardly an island left without one plastic item on its shore.

So the beautiful face of our planet reflects sparkles of plastic everywhere.

On television one can see the same on the "Housewives Of Beverly Hills". Beautiful hair, fashion, makeup, and plastic. I

Often found floating in the oceans and rivers.

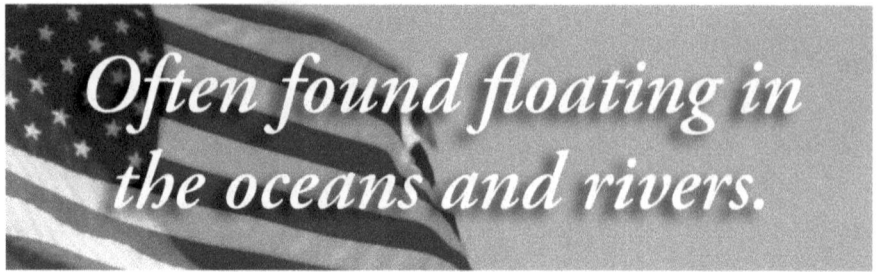

can't say they sound too intelligent either... But alas, who am I to judge? LOL.

It is also really bad on newscasters and celebrities. When they talk, something, however small, does not move. Sure pretty in touched up stills... but...?

It makes one think about how much we focus on surfaces. Values aren't important. Feelings are. Faces talk... but what about?

Old people may choose plastic.... But it really stands out the older you get. Smooth foreheads are shiny signs of misplaced effort. Real smiles and twinkles in the eye come from the enlightened, the humble and unselfish that care for others no matter how old they are.

The greatest plastic surgery pales in comparison to the giving heart. Open heart surgery is welcomed if the new heart is willing to help others quietly. The heartbeat of smooth and gorgeous souls is so attractive. Are we not drawn to those who ask nothing but to serve?? That is genuine attraction. What you get up close to is real.

Love of self is not love of others.

Put the cap back on the plastic bottle and respect the bad it can do.

Let our faces be ours, not the surgeons....

Gimme another Coke Carlos.

I'm Sorry

How many things in our pasts do we feel sorry for?

I bet it's a subject we didn't want to see coming...

Why does "sorry" seem such a difficult word?

As we get old there is that much more to have to say "I'm Sorry" for. That is ... if one is honest with one's self.

A lot of us would rather not think about saying "Sorry" to someone in the past even though something deep inside nudges us to.

And maybe all our life we are hoping a certain person would say they were sorry to us...

Just two words "I'm Sorry".

Saying I'm Sorry to someone who deserves to hear it is good.... It is even better for the person who says it. Gets something bad off their chest. You feel better. Actually you have "served" the other person with an act of humility and sensitivity. And they feel good hearing you say it. Almost like shaking hands and moving on.

Why does "sorry" seem such a difficult word?

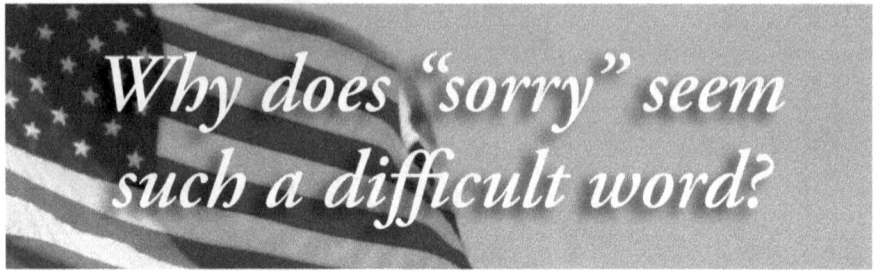

One is stronger after saying "I'm sorry". Most fear it and push it aside as they don't want to feel uncomfortable.

Some people never say they are sorry.

That is sorry for them.

Doesn't forgiveness figure into this somehow? I think we have to also forgive those who don't say they're sorry to us. That takes courage and intelligence. It's an act of giving.

Think about it.

I remember back in UDT/SEAL training there is a lovely week called "Hell Week". Maybe 8-10 hours of sleep total... maybe... and in the cold or the sand or the mud or whatever diabolic bed the Instructors created. The last day...Saturday... with zero sleep the night before is "So Solly Day". A creation meant to frighten one after all one had been through the last week. So you get hammered. And then it is over. "So Solly" for having tortured you so much.

The reward is pride and sleep.

I don't know who is sorry for what...

Only good comes from saying I'm Sorry.

Every time we do it makes us stronger....

And happier......

I'm sorry.

It's What I Do

I forgot who said that to me.

It was a statement of independence and definition.

I am who I am.

Don't try to change me.

We can be closer if you just accept me the way I am.

Maybe it is a golden retriever puppy saying with her eyes…. "It's what I do".

We accept so many things in life for what they are. No judging.

We feel good when we don't have to judge. We feel good if what we are judging to be good is good. LOL

It is criticism that is so difficult for everyone. Sometimes it is good advice…but when it's a criticism rather than advice our emotions go south.

It's all about turning a negative into a positive. There are moments that do not have to be negative. It is our choice to show the path to the positive. Our choice.

Don't try to change me.

I'd love to be the "It's what I do" person all the time.... if it was all about being good, doing good, and teaching good.

Good is positive.

Good trumps negative.

Be a puppy.

With love in your eyes.

"It's what I do".

Old Kids Matter

When you are young you look at old people as if they are just pictures on a wall or the extra guests at Thanksgiving dinner.

Ok, your parents are old but they don't count as they are only 20-30 years older.

When you are young life is so full of energy and exploration. With your whole life ahead of you, you plunge into new uncertainties, new surroundings, new people.

Danger is never seen until first tasted. Deceit and selfishness in others is initially a shock until you get used to it. Love and life and laughter and tears journey with you.

You never know what old people know until you are old (is 76 old?).

Well, guess what? The child in you never leaves. You can see what every younger generation has ahead. It's amazing. And when you meet classmates from the past you are that age again... Weird and amazing to be talking to old wrinkled-by-life faces who still have "youngs" in them. If life has not been too cruel, there is much to laugh about... and laughs from one's youth are like fine wines. You can't get enough.

Hang around old people.

When you see two old people sitting and talking together....sneak up and listen... or even better ask them respectfully if you can sit with them and join in.

You will learn the Truth about Love and the Truth about Truth.

Want a PHD in life…..?

Hang around old people.

And laugh.

Old Kids matter…

To be continued……

Global Warming

"Baby It's Cold Outside" from Louis Armstrong to Michael Buble' we sang and danced to the weather.

We have Springs, Summers, Falls, and Winters.

Seasons that create wonderful change and excitement in our lives....

Color and sounds of change....

Beauty in abundance.

Except that weather has become political. Weather has trumped war and evil. Weather is now evil as global warming threatens existence...???

Is this a political hand being played?? What about evil? What about the global rape of women? What about the global abandonment of children? What about global starvation caused by man-made atrocity politics? What in the world is the United Nations for? NYC dining and meetings??

What about global unemployment? What about global greed? What about global abandoned ethics? What about global

How about "Inner Warming"?

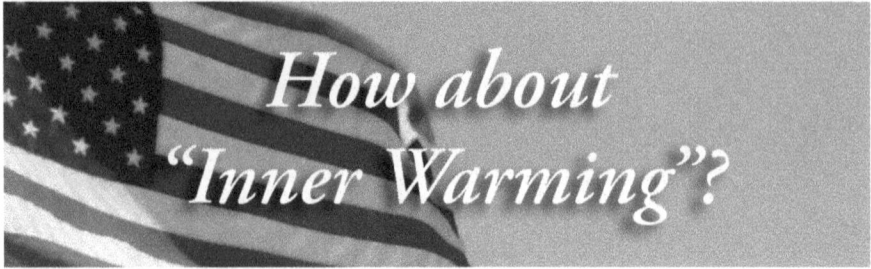

education? What about global corruption?? And on and on and on. Global warming?? Give me a break. Manage it while giving priority to all the above. Where to start??

How about "Inner Warming"?

How about getting our children to kneel and pray at their bedside? How about teaching children the difference between good and evil? That hard work and caring are the only roads to avoid extinction?

Can we find a way to put ethics and integrity back into the political system suffering from the cancer of bureaucratic chaos? Eyes should be taught to look up. The digital age has bowed young heads down to infinite keystrokes...

Churches are facing extinction.

If we continue to regulate all aspects of choice, we will have no choice. We will have overheated and burned our hearts and our very essence. This is so much more critical than the weather. Man can only be more responsible by following his heart rather than his politics.

Where is the Leader to make Truth understood by all?

When will He come?

Where will He come from?

The North Pole or our Heart....?

"Baby It's Cold Outside".

Minority Majority

Sometimes we have to go to Wikipedia to get the truth:

"Minority" is defined as "the smaller number or part, especially a number that is less than half the whole number... or ethnic minorities... or the state of being under the age of full legal responsibility"

"Majority" is defined as "the greater part, or more than half, of the total".

It so happens that our nation is founded on democratic principles where voting by individuals determines the outcome. Logically the majority wins and the regulation is passed. AKA, you don't make the runner up in the Presidential Election the President. Hello. Boards of Directors need a majority vote to go forward.

We all grow old and die and what was once our majority generation slowly becomes a minority. So, regardless, we all ultimately become a minority in the end. LOL

Today we have reshuffled the deck and created sensitivity models from which to determine the rights of minorities. Feelings count more than votes. From classrooms to the streets, feelings are to

Something is flying in the face of logic.

be protected at the expense of majorities. Bureaucratic regulation infusion makes every sensitivity a priority and abandons a majority.

We are at a nadir when any gender can choose any bathroom because of his/her feelings and sensitivities.

Something is flying in the face of logic.

Ethnic minorities do have their challenges... but only because we have lowered our standards and theirs. Crime, family breakdown, and evil have finally neutered the majority system of governance.

Old people all get it.

No one wants to listen to them because they are too old.

When they say how it was when they were growing up and things were better...

Is it really just old people talking to the wind?

Or old people who know right from wrong....?

Nonsense Sense

It is all nonsense.

Political Correctness has become nonsense.

Talking like good is bad is nonsense.

Entitlement is nonsense.

Politics is nonsense.

Pandering to sensitivities is nonsense.

No tough love is nonsense.

Bureaucracy has become nonsense.

Not confronting evil is nonsense.

Not teaching values is nonsense.

Not respecting the Flag is nonsense.

Not respecting God is nonsense.

Not knowing history is nonsense.

Beheading is nonsense.

It is all nonsense.

Not listening to old people is nonsense.

Sense out of nonsense?

Side Benefits

With a good mattress you can sleep on your side. If you've had heart surgery it's really good.

Old people have all kinds of accidents and operations so they are forced to sleep on their sides.

These days our brains need a good mattress to rest on after 24 hours of accusations, terrorism, and artfully crafted lies in the media...

Being old in the old days meant you got a little respect other than just at the Thanksgiving table.

If we don't respect the old and what they know... the cell phone abyss will swallow us up.

Why are old people avoided so much? Is it because we know all we think we need to know and don't want to be corrected??

What is cool about some cultures... aka Japan... is that the old people (I think being 76 qualifies me) are looked up to.

Hey... this old coot just checked Google and...!! In Japan there is a "Respect For The Aged Day" every Sept 15th (敬老の日, Keirō no Hi?)

There is one last side benefit....

Are they nuts??

Or are we???

In the old days the young held the door open for old people.

One of the few new blessings of being old is that you may be able to get a handicapped parking pass. She doesn't have to walk as far to TJMaxx....And you too don't when she doesn't come out in an hour...

Another, and maybe the greatest is from our great father bureaucracy which controls public transportation. Handicapped qualifies you for a wheelchair at the airport.... And that means you get wheeled past and through all the TSA security checkpoints. Going to the front of a long line makes one feel like a VIP. A Very Important Person

I bet a lot of you can't wait to be qualified!!

There is one last side benefit....

You have seen enough of life to know there has to be more.

You kneel again.

Last Laugh

Other than love, laughter is the most sought after human experience.

One could say that love is the act of the soul.

One could say that laughter is the music of the soul.

I wonder if our first gurgles as a baby are our first laughter.

Laughter is so much fun when you are young... and can help one remain forever young. It is pursued and pursued. It's really better than wrinkle cream. Who cares about wrinkles if you are always smiling??

There are some things you just can't laugh about... like other people's misfortunes and deaths.

I think making fun of self-induced mistakes is okay... People can handle criticism if you make light of it??? I do not mean the laughing-in-your face mockery.

We have had great comedians: Bob Hope, Jack Benny, Johnny Carson, Robin Williams... I bet there were comedians since day one... who helped lighten difficult times... I couldn't find any in the 1800's... need help.

We have had great comedians.

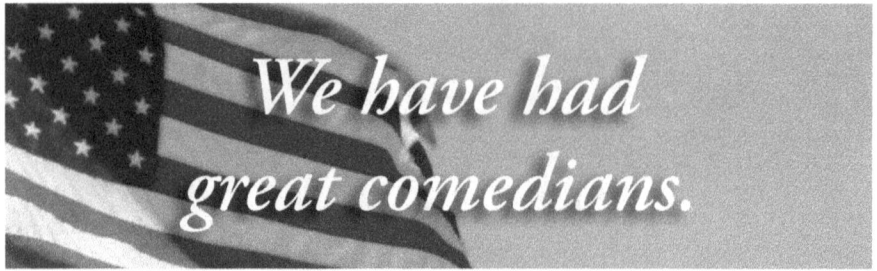

I have observed that when someone does something *not* nice to you… they don't get the last laugh. And they are the smug ones who think they did.

At the same time we reserve the right to get the last laugh on all people who do evil and who remain selfish.

Laughter punishment and laughter therapy. Take your choice.

When you find out who you were really meant to be your laughter will mean something with its innocence and compassion. Look at it this way. Helping others with laughter is serving them.

Old people just have more to laugh at as the mistakes of the younger are so funny and predictable. But this knowledge only comes with age and maturing. You gotta get old first to be sure. I am not kidding. You really don't know what you don't know until you know it. Funny? Silly? Wait and see.

You can have the last laugh if you care for others more than yourself.

Seize moments for others and laugh with them.

It's like holding hands in Heaven.

Godisnowhere

Nowhere to be found.

Search far and wide and God is nowhere to be found.

Certainly not in the news.

Certainly not in the schools.

Certainly not in the colleges.

Certainly not in the government.

We are afraid of God. God is not "politically correct". What in the world are we afraid of?? Hello??

Our traditional values and concepts of right and wrong have been marginalized. Neutered. Mocked. The same as 2,000 years ago. Go figure. Except that we can't. Minorities have taken over legalities. Are we allowing ourselves to be diminished, to be made spineless??

God still exists in some great old movies from the 1950's and a few since. Oh, yes there are some great preachers on TV... and some great preachers in churches if you take the time to find them. But that requires effort.

What in the world are we afraid of?

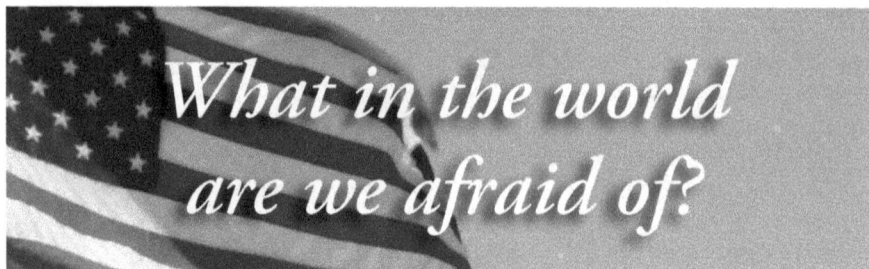

Effort these days requires mastery of cell phone and computer keyboards... "That's all folks".

Any feeling or thought can be validated by others of like mind. Truth is relative. Do you get it? Truth is no longer Truth unless validated by Wikipedia and not some silly Black Book.

I don't get it. When I look up from my cell phone and see the stars, the galaxies, and the infinity beyond. When I hold the unimaginable innocence of a new born child or a new born puppy I am forced to feel that God is somewhere. Ok, a little sin makes Him irrelevant for a moment, but just that.

Some people go to church and can't see God. They hear singing and prayer. But it seems cold and uncomfortable.... God is No Where.

Their self-confident and aimless journey continues to go nowhere. Social activities and work fill up the days' time. You don't talk about God over a drink, you talk about gossip, sports, and whatever is happening to others.

At some point, hopefully, you will figure out what is important. Something that can only be found by helping someone else. Even when you simply drive someone somewhere you feel genuine. You are helping someone.

In fact, the more ways you find to help others, the more you will find your pride increasing and your self-image improving.

Your heart will glow.

You will have let God in.

GODISNOWHERE?

GodIsNowHere

God Is Now Here.

Hair Color

When one is young the color of your hair is natural and has a unique quality that makes you... you...

We spend our entire lives trying to be different.

Trying to find a physical image that makes us more interesting... More desirable??

We spend our entire lives trying to change ourselves.

Hmmm... Life will change us regardless........

Now if one looks around... Everyone else is trying to do the same thing. We have clothing, fashion, cosmetics, lifestyles, sports... all to pursue in our quest for fulfillment.

Education should be high on the list because it helps one get closer to the Truth.

Poverty does not allow the affording of hair color, much less its maintenance. But many do succeed without makeup or degrees. Go figure.

And what is success anyway? Who defines it?? Parent, boss, friend...???

We spend our entire lives trying to be different.

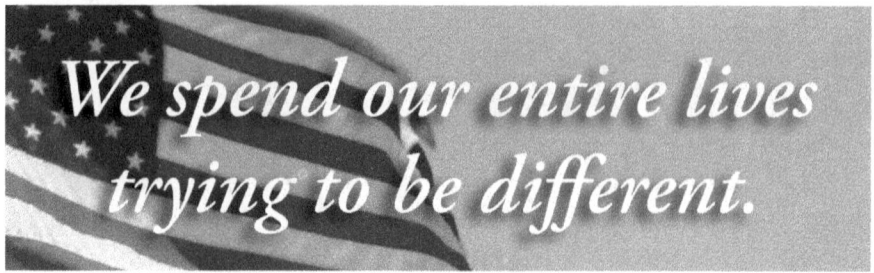

Hair highlights these days are works of art...but in a few weeks our real roots begin to show and darken the theatre... LOL

Blondes must have more fun for sure. There are more and more blondes... I always thought they were natural.... Men with colored hair just look silly. It is so obvious and so not natural looking.

Women are different. They are forced to have great looking hair to the end. The last vestige of youth seldom abandoned...except in Maine...LOL

We want to be "presentable" to others.

Maybe what a person looks like has nothing to do with who they are. You can be disfigured and be more beautiful than those with the beautiful hair. Because it is your acts which define you... not your hair. If you care for others you will be respected and quietly admired. You will know you are doing good and making a difference. Your heart will transcend all vanities.

Your heart is red and maintains its amazing uniqueness through your acts of kindness.

Listen to your heart and your face will glow.

They won't even notice you have just spent $300 on your blondeness.

They will admire the real you.

Old Puppy

He winks... pushing a cart in Costco.

Must be 90? Still thinks he is a puppy?? LOL

Golden? Black Lab?

What is it with old men and young women?

Who do we ask? Him or her?

Whose fault is it? Male or female?

Why did God create something so beautiful to begin with? You know... the puppy.

Puppies are so full of innocence and energy. They take your breath away. Bite. Bounce. Bark. Jump. Lick. The sweetest snore you will ever hear. Soon they run and swim with abandon. A symphony of youth and beauty.

Puppies.

Old puppies tend to lie asleep a lot. Old men tend to sit and look at young puppies when no one is looking. Except that everyone is. You just get caught. That is what wives are for anyway.

What is it with old men and young women?

My father-in-law was a 90 year old puppy and loved to pinch. Okay, he is excused as he was Italian….. I pinch his daughter...

Back to the mystery of life. Gender attraction. Nations fall. Generations reborn. Good and evil continue their dance. You may take sides, but if evil wins we all die and there is no love other than rape.

How is evil subdued or kept in check?

With every small act of kindness every hour of every day.

Young eyes see the goodness and are secretly emboldened to follow suit.

We will never see them replicate our act.

Have faith in all the good that you do.

Smile deep within and pinch your own bottom and bark.

Christmas Card

Open up your e-mail.

Animated Reindeer & Elves at the North Pole giving you live greetings.

Well... they move a lot.

Print from your computer.

Or watch the Three Wise Men bend over the Manger to get a look. A bright star led them there.

Or see your Facebook friends happily wishing "holiday greetings".

The bowl on the table no longer has as many Christmas Cards as last year.

It was so much fun to get the mail every day. To open the envelope and see a Christmas card signed by the friend or relative... usually with a hand written message if they were close. You could stand them up on shelves or on the dining room table and feel good.

Why are traditions being diminished or changed?

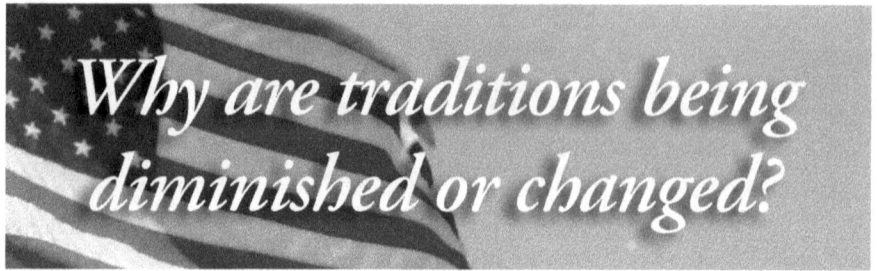

Photographs of happy family faces with children one year older.

Wonder how many snapshots it took to get all the faces looking happy and flattering? Some families are really large. It had to take an hour… But it made one feel that everyone is always happy even if some didn't like each other. You couldn't tell.

On these happiest of holidays "Happy" is wonderful… if you can afford it. Or… if you have found out who you were meant to be… wink…

You see "happy" families on lots of walls in lots of homes…. And offices…

Christmas is just before New Year's when everything starts anew.

Except that everything really started anew on the first Christmas. A faith in goodness was born.

A faith in unselfishness was born.

A faith in helping others was born.

A faith to die for was born.

Christmas cards mean that presents are coming. Christmas Eve is long because the wait for morning seems so long. Who will be the first one to the tree? Is your stocking full? Of coal? LOL.

Why are traditions being diminished or changed?

There seems to be less time for everything.

The cell phone is busy with December chatter.

No longer looking up to see the Star.

Ignorance Ignored

What you don't know won't hurt you. Huuuhh??

Suppose a Taliban was hiding behind the door?

The phrase must be reversed. What you don't know will hurt you!

No education and you understand little.

If you don't understand the right Love, you die to yourself.

There are so many teachers out there who don't belong to a union. Teachers who are not made to be politically correct.

For starters, try old people. I know they don't look like your friends and they don't move around so cool. And some can't.

Old people should be wearing t-shirts that say "been there, done that". They are so much less ignorant than you.

It's crazy that we aren't asking them for advice every moment we have. But we ignore our own ignorance... get it??

What is it about ego and vanity and insecurity that keeps the young from the old?

Of course, we never wanted our parents telling us what to do. And

Suppose a Taliban was hiding behind the door?

in later life we remember and even quote them and usually thank them for the advice.... When they are old...LOL

Ignorance breeds poverty and chaos. If you don't know what freedom is, if you don't know what injustice is, if you don't know what good is, if you don't know what ignorance is... then you are at the mercy of evil and greed. If you ignore ignorance you are doomed.

Old people usually have tried everything and ignored the one way to happiness.

It is to serve others.

To find a way to make everyone's moment you cross better.

Old people know.

They have so many stories if you would just ask....

But ask for the important ones where you can learn that your ignorance is not to be ignored any longer.

Before you dismiss God, make sure you don't do it out of ignorance... duuuhhh...

Rules of Engagement

You have met her.

Your heart skips a beat.

The eyes, the hair, the smile, the everything.

You are nervous.

You get a ring.

Never the right moment.

What are the rules anyway??? Who do you ask?? Duuuhh… try an old person.

You have held her. You are sure that she loves you… but … really enough to say yes? Suppose she says no?? Crazy stuff.

Before you engage in anything there are rules to be understood and followed unless you really do know it all… LOL.

Sometimes it should just be, screw the rules and let the moment decide. But then you have to see the parents… groan… and ask for the hand of their daughter. Her father is a terrifying hurdle. Hey…so??… ask an old person on some park bench.

What are the rules anyway???

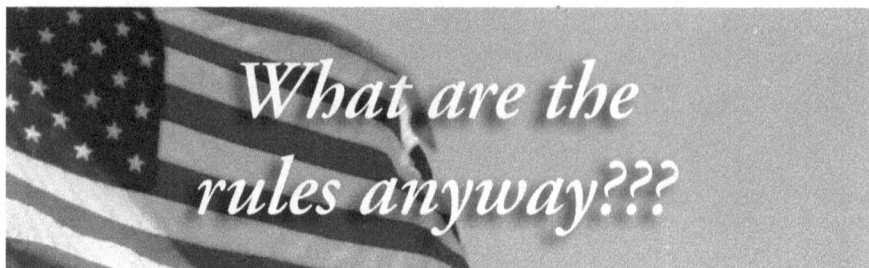

Then there is the church stuff to learn about… It's not all beer and pizza…!!! So many details… thank God the women do it…

Rules Of Engagement in the military are meant to protect lives. To avoid collateral damage. Political correctness has been driving decision making today. The delay of layers of approval have taken the edge off surprise and put our soldiers at risk. Opportunity has little patience with delay. You are not getting engaged to a fiancée, you are pulling the trigger on someone who has no business being there unless he knows the risks. The enemy is not dumb. Evil is not dumb. They must not win. They will if the ROE takes the decision away from the moment.

Rules, rules, rules.

How many officers and politicians and bureaucracies and lawyers manage the rules to ultimately cover their asses?

There is a cultural war going on.

On the internet and in places like the Middle East.

At one point the sergeant has to say all rules are off… win right now or die!

Enemy Power

You have a cause?

You have an enemy.

Deep with us all is the sense of right and wrong.

It nags us silently until we yield.

There are more valid causes than you could list in a lifetime, be they private or of the world. We fight for causes. They define an enemy. Fighting for what is right is an impulse since the beginning. The problem comes when the cause is self-serving or a false creation.

Today, every cause gets headlines and loud proponents. Minority causes get priority. Sick causes are seen as worthy. Majority causes are suspect.

"Be-Cause"… Be a Cause and somehow you go to heaven? A martyr for a cause? Verbal bombs strapped to the cause vest. Angry signs and threats. The networks can't keep up with them. 'Cause there is a Cause Cancer metastasizing.

Create an enemy and you get power.

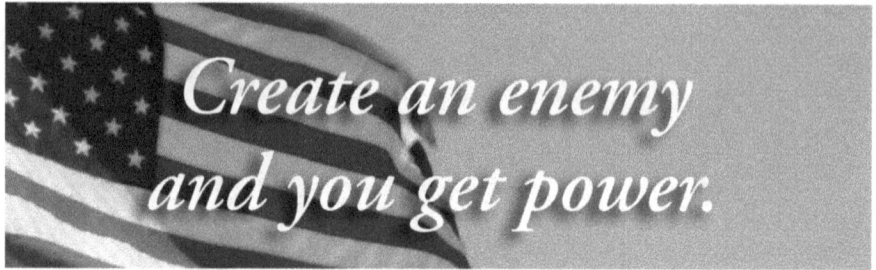

Create an enemy and you get power. However, the enemy does too...?? Crazy riddle if you follow it.

Causes aren't the enemy... WE are... when we cling to false priorities. The arctic ice coverage has expanded 50% since 2012. Poverty, greed and corruption continue to increase.

What are the important causes??? Everyone should have a list... then they should go into a database so we can actually see our priorities. NBC/NY Times/CNN Gallup can then tell the truth.

My priorities (causes) are:

My family

My employees

Honesty (in Government too)

Education (values, respect, responsibility, patriotism)

Attacking evil

Attacking mediocrity

Attacking poverty

See... mine are different than yours. But I am an old person which allows a different level of discernment. I don't know it all...

but do have a better understanding of what doesn't work.

Causes are defeating common sense. Minorities are defeating majorities.

Evil causes are desecrating the Middle East and elsewhere…..

We have to look to Heaven to find the cause of all the causes.

Are we a defective cause?

I want my Cause to frighten evil.

All in???

Midcourse Correction

Hey…watch out!!!

The bridge is down!!!

What does the GPS say?

How are we going to get there now?

You hope this happens as early in life as possible. That you realize that the path chosen goes nowhere.

Hey… like dishonesty, self-priority, substance & truth abuse… and on and on…

It is never too late to make a correction in who you are. How in the world can you find out who you were meant to be if you don't avoid the fruitless paths?

"Who cares about who I was meant to be" says the fool. If you don't end up making other's lives better then you will never know. If one does not find humility, then one will never know. It takes courage to find out where you should be going.

Deep inside we all have a moral GPS. It is constantly sending us private messages like "turn right" not "left"… LOL… When

What does the GPS say?

we stop ignoring them and maybe check with a good old person, preferably a church goer, we can get help.

GPS??? God Protects Souls?

Success comes from changing plans. Success comes from perseverance. Success comes from being honest with one's self. Success comes from serving others.

The enemy can secretly move into a position to ambush you. The enemy wants to own you. The enemy wants to kill you. You should always have spies to warn you. Intelligence that is intelligent. You must ambush evil instead. Why are we so lazy about doing more good?

We can help the world only if we are strong first.

I think a mid-course correction for our nation has to be made. Bureaucracy has stifled initiative and opportunity. Politics has become ingrown and inefficient and corrupt....

"Helmsman!! Hard turn to the right 180 degrees. Steady as she goes"... "We'll not let this storm go over our bows." "Carry on."

We have to find the courage to do this with our lives...

Correct in midcourse.

It's never too late.

Your captain may be old…. But who cares…. He knows.

"All ahead full."

Human Cathedral

She teared up in front of me.

A 7th grade teacher.

I told her what I am trying to do.

I told her about when my mother and I would kneel at bedside and pray… "Now I lay me down to sleep…"

Looking back now I realize that that changed my life.

Thank you Mom, thank you.

I didn't get it until now. You don't have to go to church to pray. It is just you and God anywhere in the world at any moment. Prayer dignifies the moment and nourishes one's understanding of right and wrong. It is more than conscience…

Church is great for many. But for many it is intimidating. That's really okay. Churches have inspired preachers who can reach you deep within. And many who don't. If you don't find the right one for you, then you must move on until you do.

There can also be friends who you trust… friends who act unselfishly… who matter. Paths can cross anywhere in the world

But for many it is intimidating.

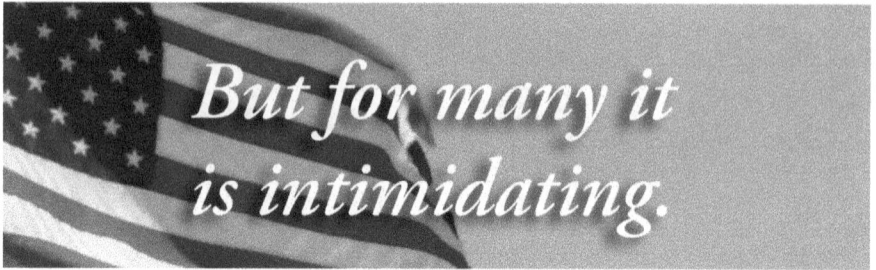

and spiritual magic can happen. A spiritual connection that forces you to look up and ponder the infinite. Hands go limp, cell phones drop, and fingers intertwine in prayer.

I had the honor of being asked to give the keynote address on Veteran's Day 2016 to 600 students and veterans in a church. As a former Navy Frogman my life's journey led me to this moment.

I gave them all I had.

I served their moment.

And it all started with a "Now I lay me down to sleep…"

Hope you are watching Mom.

Up Periscope

50 years ago, I remember locking out of an old diesel sub, USS SEA CAT. Locking out is when you leave a submerged submarine through an escape trunk; a double hatch cylinder that will fit 2 men with scuba tanks and gear. Then... swim off on a mission to return later at night.

The way things are going these days, Christianity is withdrawing to some safe and less seen quarters. The onslaught of criticism from the liberal, all knowing, elite has weakened the nation and the world.

My friend Ted used this analogy of us staying submerged below the surface for protection and comfort.

But what is a person supposed to do in life? Hide from reality? Wars of all sorts will still have to be fought. They will use up our young in greater quantity the longer we delay seeing the Truth.

So... Up Periscope America (UPA). Look at what is happening in the streets. The imprisoned black and the intellectually arrogant white are in their own submarines. Waging cultural war. And they don't have a periscope.

Be the periscope in your family.

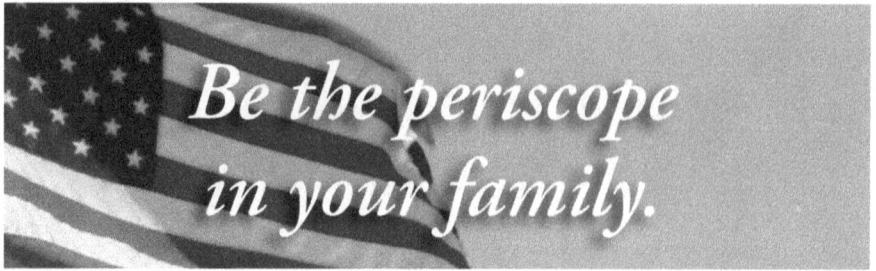

So, once again, we old people should disavow comfort and make a difference. Doesn't age infer wisdom? I know we all have strong opinions forged from adversity and mistakes.

Stand up. You only have to do it one person at a time. Express your beliefs and opinion. They have value. Tell a young person. Do not be timid… They need to feel sincerity and passion. They are so hungry for it. They look down into their cell phones for validation of every nonsensical notion they have. We know what is going on.

The Love of Truth and the Truth of Love should be ammunition enough.

Put one other person in your sights once a week until you can do it once a day.

Be the periscope in your family.

Then surface.

And look at your bubbles…

The Label

She was fixated on the lady in front of her.

It was a nice dress.

But the label was sticking up.

An insignificantly ponderous moment.

What to do??

Nothing to worry over?

Except she did?

Why, in heaven's name bother??

Nobody around her knew what she was thinking.

She wanted to politely tuck the label in for the lady.

Was it impertinent to tell her what she wanted to do?

Such an insignificant moment.

Such an insignificant choice.

Why all the private fuss?

She was fixated on the lady in front of her.

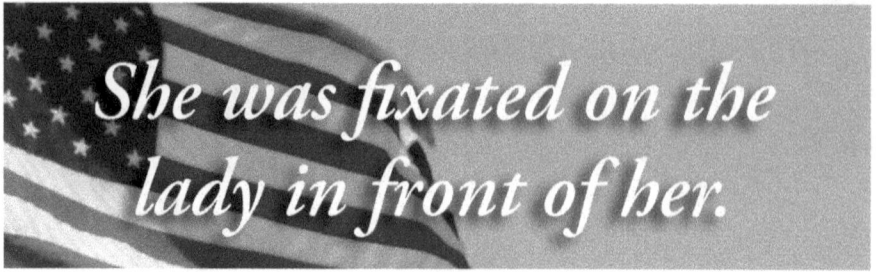

To do one very small act to help another?

To risk embarrassment.

Would you want someone to graciously tuck yours in?

So you don't look silly for hours?

It's just a label.

It's just a person.

It's just a choice that tells who you are…

The Baton

Baton?

What is that?

Is it the thing they pass on in a relay race?

Like the 4 x 100? 4 x 400?

At a precise moment when a runner or swimmer has all but exhausted himself… Composure and focus must be exact as the baton is handed to your teammate. Not a wobbly pass, but a steady and firm placement into the awaiting hand that is not looking. The next sprinter cannot lose a second in the pass…..

To win is the goal. Every second counts.

Is life a race? To be able to afford a great car? To be able to buy fun, dinners, and entertainment? Is life a race to get promoted? Is life a race to figure out what life is? Do we really ever try? "What's it all about Alfie?"

We depend on so many people in life. Do they depend on us? Are their knowledge-batons worth passing on to children, to grandchildren, to great grandchildren?

Is life a race?

If we have no baton, then our life has little meaning to anyone but our selves. When it is over. We are over. Makes it seem pointless.

But what about all the good we finally learned about? Like what is right and what is wrong... what leads somewhere and what is a dead-end blind alley.

What about Truth and what about Love? Where should we be heading? Each person must decide what race they want to be in. Lasting peace and fulfillment? If not, close this book and come back when you are sufficiently bruised...

The race is personally won when we are able to pass on knowledge that we know, that we really know is good. It's called values 101. What is really valuable?

Our gift to our grandchildren's grandchildren should be what will keep them from harm, from making the same mistakes we did. This is what fantastic is. Serving others is what fantastic is. Making anyone... any stranger feel a little better... that you did not judge them... that you increased their self-respect and self-worth. This is what fantastic is.

The baton has to be more than....."Hi, how's it going?" or that loving question... "What's up?"

It's for us to figure out and pass on… the baton.

Of Truth and Love.

We spend our whole lives trying to find it…

When it was always beneath our left breast…….

Immune Systems Matter

I have lived this long not because everything is germ free, but because my immune system was healthy and intolerant of attack.

I have successfully developed antibodies which win the battle over germs...

All of a sudden everything must be sanitized

I feebly work out in the hospital wellness center. People are either spraying or wet towel wiping machines before and after they exercise. They are killing the germs I need to make my antibodies. My antibodies love germs... They eat them like we do pizza.

This folly is even more amusing as the sanitizer wipers are just doing stupid spots... What about all the doorknobs? It would make a great video watching them do a half-ass job of killing my germs.

Now, let's get serious. Government has been sanitizing everything that is important. In its bureaucratic wisdom of self-preservation it passes thousands of rules so no one can make a mistake. Except they are making the biggest mistake by regulating basic freedoms. We learn from our mistakes. You can't sanitize man. You can't sanitize business.

I love the smell of disinfectant.

The small business is the immune system for our economy. Churches are the immune systems for our values.

Our values are being sanitized by media, celebrities, and politicians. Basic ethics are being compromised in the double speak on the TV screen. In the mad chase for news the negative has become the dominant message. The next murder, the next slander, the next intrusion into privacy, the next half-truth not validated. All of these are attacking our traditional values and basic rights.

Wipe me.

I love the smell of disinfectant.

GPS

New Year's Eve is when we all, not too soberly, make resolutions to improve our self and our direction.

All in laughter and merriment except that change always has to be addressed so we don't become wanderers in our own space.

GPS.

Global Positioning Satellite. Helps us with maps and voice prompts to get us to a selected destination. They really work. They really help jets get us to Disneyland or missiles find their targets.

There is no longer any excuse for getting lost.

Except that most people are and don't know it. Deep inside there is this quiet, private stirring of insecurity. We do our best to gloss over it with needs and wants and attractions that busy our spirit and keep us from focusing on what we may really need.

So how about a different take on GPS? Geo Personal System? To get a satellite to beam us answers? To help us ease our ignored pain. Drugs are often used rather than GPS. GPS requires an open mind… and maybe an open heart…??? GPS means there

So how about a different take on GPS?

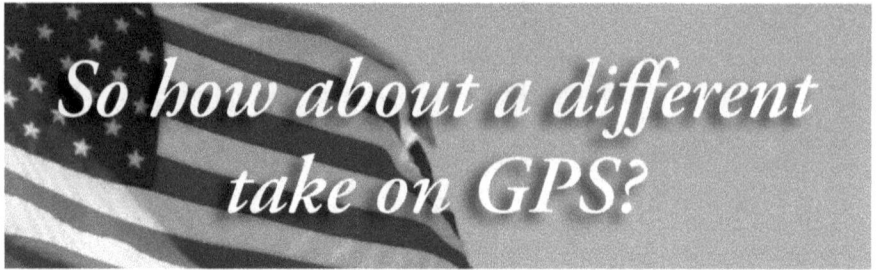

has to be a person to go to for advice. Who has travelled down the road of mistake and hurt. Who knows what real good and what real evil is. More than likely this person will be old. We "oldies" are often ignored by the young when we actually have more to give than all their Facebook and cell phone advisors. It is scary that so much knowledge goes untapped.

And lastly, there is another satellite that is really there beyond the galaxies beyond the black holes in our universe. So far beyond that even the scientists have no answers. What is the equation for infinity anyway? If you want to be lazy, then don't search. If you want to be lazy then accept the skepticism of the enlightened nay-sayers. They even say that evil is a psychological aberration and can be dismissed with regulations. The feelings of the victim are not as important as the sad excuse of the criminal. We have to feel sorry for the criminal first….. First Amendment??

You know…. when you witness someone being kind you privately smile. Why? When you see someone be rude to another you feel disappointment. Good trumps evil in the private world of the heart.

I contend that there is a road to find that is called Good Street. It is narrow and hard to find. Quitters will remain imprisoned in their doubt and insecurity. The funny thing about Good Street is that once you are on it anything is possible.

Your potential is unleashed.

Just grab the Black Book and GPS yourself with the God Positioning Satellite.

Why not?

It's only your life…

The Envelope

One envelope in the mailbox.

The hand pauses.

Who is it from?

From WWI to today the letter from home or the letter to home was waited for as if it were a million dollars of gold. "Love Mom" or "Love Danny" went straight to the heart.

What was in the envelope, the letter… was all that mattered….

Today there is facebook and skype. It is still hard to imagine talking on video live to your son in the military in real time. Simply amazing!

Is the paper letter dead?

Only if we are.

Letters need to be sent that enclose our private Love and our private Truth. All that we have learned with age. Letters must be written to the generations to come. To your great, great, great grandchildren. There must be something that you have learned that is worthwhile?? If not a lot?? Come on… don't be falsely

Is the paper letter dead?

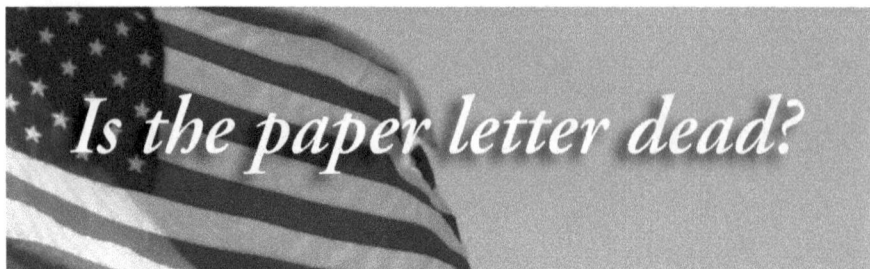

humble. Isn't there something you wished your mother or father had told you? A mistake that could have been avoided? Or maybe what good and evil really are? How to avoid dead-end streets??

Imagine an envelope you could open from you great grandfather telling you that doing something for another person is the most important thing in life?? A lot to think about? Possibly influencing your whole life??

If you were a GI in WWII you jumped up when your heard the "Mail Call" bell. Ran to see if you got anything. And if you got a letter you ran to some private place to cherish it like caviar.

The envelope.

Many envelopes are what we should fill with love. Advice… yesss… But given in love… We should all write them. It is a good feeling to write about what is good to pass on to future generations. Maybe write them every month or at least every year. You will learn about yourself.

Can you envision 200 years from now a young person opening an old box in some attic and seeing your envelope?? Opening and feeling your love from 200 years ago??

Go ahead.

Write it.

Nobody has to know.

Love Dad.

Oxygen Bottle

Pure O2.

Gotta have oxygen to survive on sea, air, land, and space.

No O2.

No you.

I am now around the O2 bottle generation much more than when I was younger. A man's gotta breathe!!! In fact, we all fight for oxygen all our lives. Suffocation is not to be played with. Nor is life….

First responders leap to your side with an O2 bottle. Blood has to have oxygen to be blood…. Hearts pump blood so we can make our existence have meaning….

Our first breath. Can't remember?? That's ok… no one can…. But look how important it was… I was a blue baby for 6 months….

Once upon a time as a young man I was trained to swim on pure O2. To sneak into harbors and help ships come to premature ends…. Aka …sink them. Our Emerson O2 Rebreathers gave off no bubbles so we could not be detected….

Gotta have oxygen to survive.

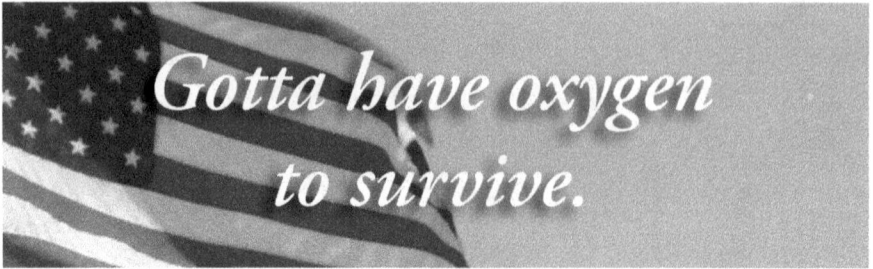

Then again pilots can go high where there is little oxygen and survive off their O2 bottles.... Astronauts have taken their O2 with them to the moon and back.

Yet, oxygen can be deadly. You don't want it around fire.... as Apollo 1 tragically found out. Tragically. God bless them.

On our commercial jets we are assured O2 masks will drop from the overhead.

Military freefall HALO guys (High Altitude Low Opening... or HAHO... you can figure it out)... leap into the blackness at 30,000 feet with their 02 bottles affixed.

I look at my friend old Sal at the wellness center. He gets from his wheelchair to the treadmill with his O2 bottle standing by.... In case he falls....

But... there is more to life than oxygen. It is what you do with this gas, this fuel, to make life have meaning.

It's not the O2 dummy, it's the heart...

It's whether you listen to it and help others who need assurance and affirmation.

Others who need to know what the Truth is.

Who need to be shown how to help others.

I hope that on my last breath I am helping someone.

Thank you O2, now I can turn blue…

Hallmark Channel

Channel 385 down here.

Never, ever, thought I would watch it.

When wifey turned it on I was gone to spy stuff, revenge, killing, detectives and the like downstairs. The British have some amazingly sophisticated detective series. Crazy good.

Then there are sports. Then there is the news. NBC, ABC, CNN, Fox, MSNBC and 10 others trying to make half-truths exciting and urgent. We buy into it. Any minority group, aka 3 people on a street corner with signs and cheeseburgers, get coverage… and their cause gets recognition…. The majorities have refined the art of invisibility and allowed the minority issue its gravitas. We are getting what we deserve.

Can't someone make goodness into a minority cause so it gets some exposure??

Can't we make every value a cause? Inundating the media with what is right and wrong? Good and evil? How about just 3 people for God? Claiming their rights and protesting in front of the ACLU while causing pedestrian disruption?? LOL.

Never, ever, thought I would watch it.

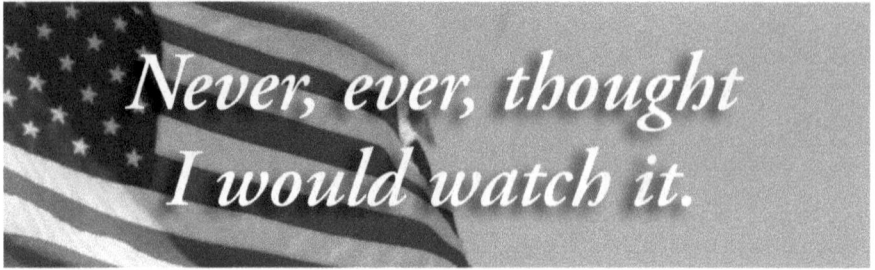

I agreed to watch one Hallmark Christmas movie with my wife. I was all ready to criticize, moan, and groan. Then the oddball guy caught the eye of the already engaged little cutie and I waited for the commercial break to leave. But… I just had to see the next scene to be sure the new love would have a chance. I got hooked and had to make it to the end. I now love "love stories" with happy endings. It sure beats the heck out of watching the supreme bad guy take it in the forehead from the good-guy sniper rifle a mile away.

Love trumps death now.

Whenever I hear "honey, the new Hallmark Movie is starting"….

I rush to brush my teeth, grab some water and polar fleece and pillow and sit where I am told.

During commercial breaks I flick back to Fox News.

Just to see what is important.

Old Dog

New Tricks?

The saying is that you can't teach them….

Well, when my dogs get old I ask nothing new of them. Their loyal eyes just look as innocent as they did as puppies. Raised on reciprocal love they win. They teach you that the trick of love is loyalty and trust.

I lie down and hold the paw for their last breath. As close as I can be to the love they gave to me.

Some of us are old dogs now. We want someone to hold our hand for our last breath too. Well… it would be nice…

Who is to say you can't learn new tricks regardless of age? Change is possible to the end. New humility can be found. New generosity or caring can be created. The trick is to realize that you are only as important as the people you help to smile, as the people you help to help themselves. To the people you help to learn to forgive, to the people young or old to whom you teach a new trick. Tricking them into wanting to do good, to recognize evil in its smallest manifestation.

Some of us are old dogs now.

I'm an old dog now. My bark is much worse than my bite. But I can still bark warnings, and bark them sooner. I can't run or swim like I used to. But my pointers can make a difference. Old people are good pointers. They have been there.

It should be an honor for a young person to know an old person they can trust.

All we want to be is your old dog looking into your eyes…

Sleeping by your side…

Guarding you from the tricks of life.

Age Less

If you go to Paris and the Louvre you will see paintings that have never aged.

Rembrandt, Van Gogh, Monet...and on and on...

You can go back thousands of years and find art that is still revered. Crazy. They never aged.

Of course, thousands of years from now selfies on Facebook will probably be out there in celestial databases. But there is still nothing like oil on canvas. No comparison!!

Today we are bombarded by our ever-caring media outlets with aids to not aging. From body to skin to brain we are promised tools to slow down visual aging. We buy into it. Spending fortunes. Probably more than needed to feed every hungry child for life.

We don't want to age. But if we have to... we want to age less. It is like we want to be remembered for our looks...??

Exercise sure enhances the quality of life and youthful vigor. I am just finding it harder to embrace now that I am old.

We don't want to age.

You can hang around young people… but they don't want to hang around you as much…. They are dancing to the music of eternal freedom…. except that 50 years later the music is slower…..

It is November 30, 2016 and Christmas is 25 days away. All our lives we remember what a special day it was when we were young. The decorations joyfully signaling that there will be presents under a Tree. Somehow at Christmas, for that brief moment, we are ageless.

It is even more fun finding gifts for more people that one would have thought. There are more people in your life to thank than you think. One does not have to wrap with festive paper and ribbon the gifts that mean the most.

I feel young when I am kind.

I feel young when I hug someone.

I feel young when I make someone smile.

I feel young when I say "God Bless You".

And this all started in a barn in a manger?

Ageless………….

Beach Boys

I have a friend who is still alive that is still friends with one of the Beach Boys....

I was in the Navy at the time they got famous. With some roots in LA, I was all excited about this new surfing subculture. Music helps cultures form.

My friend had lost his parents in an automobile incident as a youth. I never knew a guy who could just start talking to a stranger so fast. Seemed like they were old friends in minutes. My wife is kinda that way too. Her childhood was also broken. Amazing individuals coming from places we will never know. Resilience, perseverance??? For most it does not work out. Don't know that there are any statistics.

I'll never forget diving in Catalina with my friend.

How do we ever last this long? How does this uniqueness remain? Even to this day, as whatever iteration of the Beach Boys remains, their uniqueness defies mortality. They can die and their music can still be heard.....

The same really goes for us. When we help someone we are

Music helps cultures form.

creating another kind of music. It too, will never die....it will be passed on however sublimely. Others know....

"With A Song In My Heart"... a song from a Rogers & Hart 1929 musical kinda gets to the heart of who we can be.

Can you imagine others privately humming your song, the memory of an unselfish act you helped them with? That is "The Sound Of Music" that we can forever be remembered for. Not the selfish things we have done....but the good.

Our music.

Our beat.

Hey........... "outside"......

"Surfin' USA."

Humility Rocks

Humility rocks.

Let's clear the air right up front.

This is not about a variant of the Pet Rock.

And it is much more expensive.

All our lives we are bombarded with things we need. Ad after ad after ad. Celebrities having all this fun with their fame and money. All you hear about them is all they are doing and all they have. Of course... they get their paparazzi. LOL. Everything they do is reported by the media.

They must spend fortunes to find privacy.

If you want to be famous, you can. You certainly can go down the "self" road. You can be talked about as much as you want. Say unfair things about someone and you dominate the moment. You can bask in your own spotlight and smile in the mirror. You can criticize Christianity and become famous.

But does all this self-induced notoriety last? Or is it discarded by the newest gossip?

You can rock…but can you roll???

You can rock…but can you roll??? LOL…. Roll into the future???

Humility is the most subconscious attribute one can find. It is seldom talked about. Maybe because one is not sure one's self is humble. So… it is avoided in conversation… Hmmm??

Humility infers a quiet going on about your business. By not bringing attention to yourself.

In fact, it means not even being aware of yourself.

In fact, it means doing little for yourself and a lot for others.

To really make a difference you help others.

You will be talked about for years.

Every small unselfish act makes you an invisible celebrity to the person you helped.

Even one kind word can put a smile inside some other person.

Humility means you aren't even thinking about it.

Maybe a handshake or wink when appropriate… But that's all….

You can't search for humility.

It just has to happen without you knowing it.

Your self becomes boring.

Helping others is a blast.

Humility Rocks.

Love Object

Have you ever been a love object?

What did it feel like?

Is being loved different than being a love object?

We all love objects.

How about a Chanel handbag or a red Ferrari....?? They are expensive love objects for many. Few will ever have them.... And anyway... then what?? The more expensive something is, generally the less it is used.

Would you rather own a love object? Or be the object of love?

Owning a love object is kinda a dead-end street. The pursuit is exciting. Some just keep pursuing and end up with impressive collections to impress. But where is love?

We all want someone to love us. We try so many schemes to find it. We adjust our looks to attract. We go places to find attraction. All with the hope of finding more than superficial love.

It is a crazy swirling of "ME's" if looked down upon from space.

We all want someone to love us.

The mating circus of the genders… LOL

To be loved you have to love. To find love you have to love. Real love means sacrificing self for another. Think about it… The love object has to be more important than yourself. The person being loved has to have total Trust to love in return. How do you do that?

Your life has to be less important than the loved. Serving others is love. Serving does not mean waiting on their table. It means putting self in second place. All the time. Every day.

Make everyone else an object of your unselfish love. Old people finally get it and find peace. Let the grandkids know you love them every chance you get. Not with presents mailed but with words and a hug.

Make the object of your love produce a smile.

Smiles last longer than cars.

Rocking Chair

Have you ever been to Cracker Barrel?

They serve fantastic down-to-earth food at great prices.

Country store atmosphere...

For some reason, you feel at home when you enter the front door.

Oh... they also sell old fashioned wood rocking chairs for $75 to $350 on their front porch. Sitting down on one is like being in a time machine.

The darn things work... no springs... you just rock and worries seem to be left in the car. Looking at a rocking chair you can see the structure, the pieces, how they connect, and how you will feel in it. And you are right. It is no more than it appears to be and delivers everything you want from it. Escape. Just rock and take in the surroundings, looking at earth from your rocking orbit. No need for a Saturn 5 booster to get you somewhere where you can look down on earth in awe.

Today, nothing is as it seems. You need a cell phone and Google to find out what something is. Google NASA and view the endless galaxies and... the crazy beauty of earth. From the rocking chair

Have you ever been to Cracker Barrel?

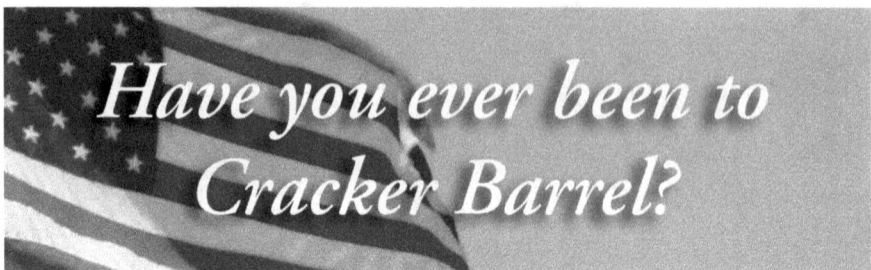

on a farmer's porch the farmer could use his telescope and see the heavens and be left with the same conclusion. That the majesty of the stars defies comprehension. No need to get to orbit.

Today, we are told the truth, supposedly…, from "reality" shows on TV. Except they are a staged false reality. News and entertainment shows abound in unimaginable variations. Few not distorting truth. Sure… bad guys get killed… and good girls find their prince…. But the illusion of dreams keep us from finding our real dreams. And the life we were meant to have.

When life was simpler, Truth was easier to see. Good and bad choices were clearer. Journeys were easier to map. Finding out that helping others made your life a reality show with meaning and purpose.

Pretending to be good took too much energy.

Being unselfish was so much easier.

Think about it.

In a rocking chair.

Honey-Do

Guys don't talk about it.

But if you listen carefully you will hear them all whisper the feared term "honey-do".

The honey-do list is compiled most of the time on the spur of the moment… You gotta be quick. And as you get older and slower….? LOL

It is our job as warriors to protect the family and wife. It is the wife's job to keep everyone busy… then she can supervise… then she can hold you accountable.

"Honey", how would you like to go shopping with me at Best of Everything?? "Sure dear… I'd love to do that. They have chairs outside…" You have agreed to "do" a "do". Get it?

We just missed having a wife become president where she could have exercised her "honey-do" powers. A lot of government needs to be told what to do. Let's see how it works out. LOL.

The fact of the matter is we should not have to be told what to do. There are important matters and chores that must be acted on immediately. Maybe, "just do it" before one is asked.

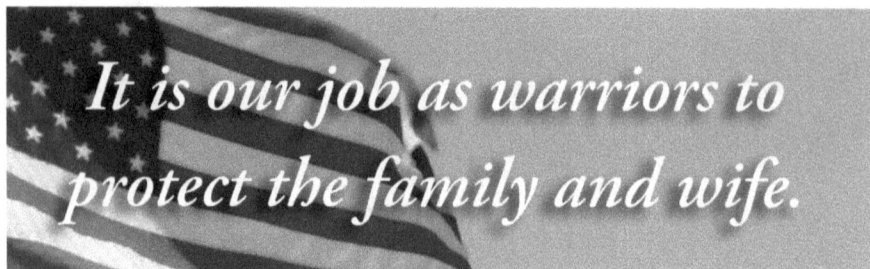

It is our job as warriors to protect the family and wife.

There is the obvious…. But more important is the non-obvious… until it is…LOL

We must be able to see the small ways we can help someone and act in the moment. A helping hand or a helping word must be our saber. Ready for use in an instant. Our own honey-do list must be reflexive. It can be, but only if one knows the Truth. That standing up for Good defines manhood.

Find out what evil is. Find out what good is. Make your own set of values based on good. Then defend them. Every moment of every day is an opportunity to prove you are bigger than yourself.

How about "Honey, how about I go shopping with you?"

"Honey-do" yourself.

Be busy with *your* "honey-dos".

Make them have meaning.

Follow your heart.

"Please… honey."

If Only

"If only."

How many times have you heard that?

How many times have you told yourself that?

"If only I had known that" I would have done it differently.

Except that many things done wrong or incorrectly cannot be changed and become part of one's uniqueness if a lesson was learned. A lesson is really a class on doing something right. The classroom is in your brain. "Lesson learned".

Lessons learned are taught in the military, in medicine, and in life… They must be passed on so others benefit. Everyone has private lessons learned… which become meaningless if not shared. We must share them. Especially us old people. This is how we matter. We can save lives by just passing on one truth, one lesson learned.

Life is a classroom. When we are young we goof off. When we are young we think we know everything. We have no clue as to the complexities of pain and suffering and indifference. We seldom choose to make a difference until our hair turns grey and

The classroom
is in your brain.

some sense from observations and lessons learned sink in. The "aha" moment. Yet it is not that simple. "Aha" means nothing if you don't pass it on.

Even a letter to your future grandchildren's grandchildren.

Think about it.

Lessons learned?

If only I had written that letter…

Antique Shopping

I didn't know what antique shopping meant until I became one.

How can you appreciate old things when you are not old??

All this fuss about things from the past.

Antiques can cost a fortune depending on what store you find them in. Of course, there is the flea market and the yard sale that can harvest some of the finest antiques. Designers just paint them in some special color and the price goes up and up and up. HGTV is a great place to see how antiques can be updated and used in remodeling homes. A lot of fun playing with antiques.

I just wish someone would play with me... LOL. When you are dead you can no longer play "antique".

So... we have established that things from the past can have value. There are the pyramids of Egypt to the paintings throughout Europe. Every nation in the world has old things to revere, respect, and care for. When they are plundered part of our soul is taken whether we know it or not.

For an antique to have value it must be respected first. Its history

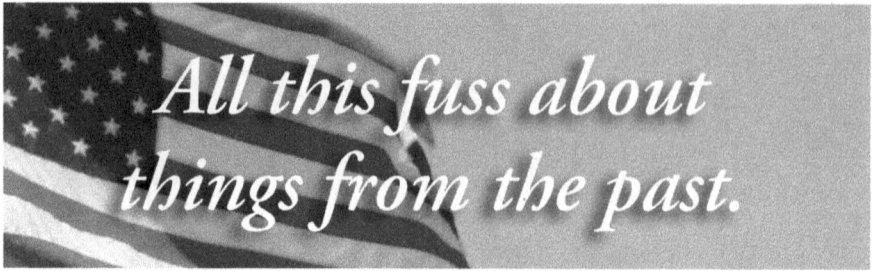

is important. The same goes for us. Are there things to be learned from old people?? Try asking and you will be amazed.

Every old person has a story that must not die unread. How we are built is more mysterious than the Pyramids. There are secret passages that can take one to special places. We must explore and take risks in these unknown territories. Antique hunting? We must not let their riches just be ashes and not unlocked.

So next time you see an old "antique" person, sit down next to them with respect and find out more about their journeys and what they think is important.

You may discover something that is invaluable.

Knowledge that you cannot buy.

A lot of them walk early in the morning.....

That's a place to start Antique Shopping.

Extra Crispy

KFC started it all.

They are to blame.

They should get the Pulitzer Prize for National Girth.

What is it about extra crispy that is so gooood??

Men always look for things that might be extra crispy on menus. From the finest to the least expensive. It is usually the least expensive that create real crispy and thrive. Crunch rules. LOL

Bacon, meats, anything with skin can participate in the crispy revolution. The heck with weight. The flavor and the crunch in the moment rule. Don't let them put sauce on the General Tsao Chicken… you do it… to preserve the crispy…. Preserve The Crispy. PTC sounds like a potential political movement. Sensitivity focused. Our need for crispy protected.

Skin deep? Some of us old people have spent a lot of time in the sun. Some are weathered. Some just wrinkled. We tend to judge them by their skin…. Their looks.

Can you judge a chicken by its skin? Undercooked? Overcooked?

What is it about extra crispy that is so gooood??

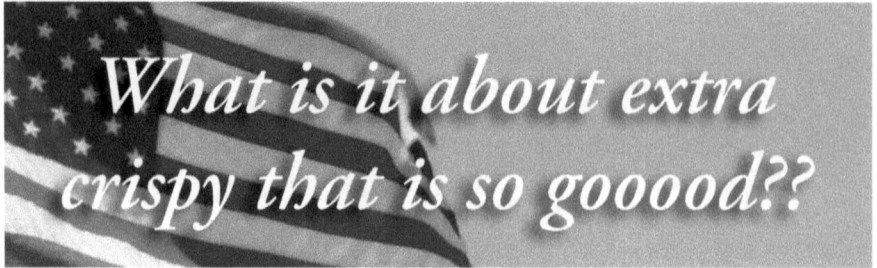

Sometimes life turns out fried. Too much heat, too many mistakes and persons have quit. We say their brains are fried…. Something wrong with the recipe?

It takes a Chef to get everything just right… so that "extra crispy" is a delicacy. KFC has their recipe tuned to a science. The rules are so tight. If you don't follow them then your franchise is closed. Their rules are good. They produce really good chicken. Drive through too…

The same holds for people.

If they follow the 10 Commandments.

Just Say No

"What is it about "No" you don't understand?"

"Yes Sir." "No Sir." "Yes Sir." "No Sir."

It gets repeated ad nauseam in the military… until you get it.

Yes means yes and no means no. Black and white. If you whine or dispute it means 200 pushups or an hour run in the sand… over and over until you get it. Pain is the deciding factor. No pain no gain. Pain brings clarity… eventually.

With good parents discipline gives "No" meaning. And we learn if there is a price. Today's kids are enabled to say no and get away with it so their feelings are not hurt. Rubbish. And that is what they become when they feel entitled.

No is a special word. It can save lives. Old people know No. They have gone through life's initiation process. All have made choices that ignored the "No" within.

We have allowed a generation of no "No's" to thrive. When No is said to them, they check their cell phones for support and ignore the No.

Yes means yes and no means no.

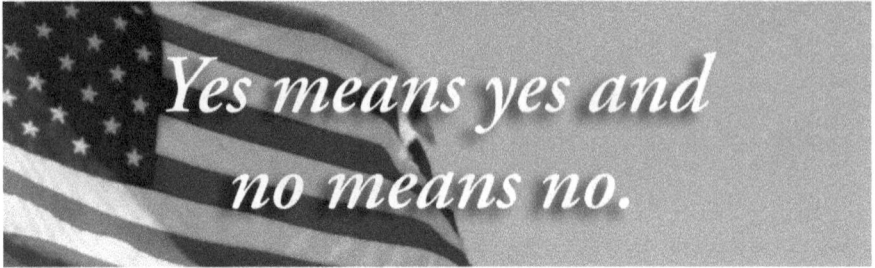

Is it time we as a people say No in a way that has the world believing it?

How to learn it before it is too late? Try a few years in the military and learn respect and the good of the No. Good rules followed are so cool.

Now if you don't have the courage to enlist... then find a good old person fast and at least have the courage to ask him to help you understand things. You can prevent so much personal pain and hurt to others.

If someone will not accept a valid No, then we must walk away.

Tough love.

Rock bottom must be found by some before they stop looking down to their cell phones....

And... look Up to the only Yes.

Save My Heart

Let's talk heart-to-heart.

One can if there is trust.

But most of the time trust is not there and fake conversations ensue.

When you fall in love you feel that heart-to-heart connection and talk as if there is no tomorrow. Heart to heart. Exciting and alive. Life at its best.

It seems that the heart is at the center of everything. No heart and you get evil, you get war, you get cruelty, you get indifference, you get hunger, and you get nowhere. Game over. The world we hoped for ends....

Circumstances, addictions, broken families, dishonesty... all wage wars against trust.

Without trust, there is no communication.

Hearts have to talk.

Hearts are broken when they are alone. Homeless.

Let's talk heart-to-heart.

Is a heart worth saving? Should a soldier dive on a grenade to save his buddies?

What is worth saving to save a heart? Would you like your heart to be saved? At someone else's expense. Tough choice.

Old people know about it. The homeless who hit rock bottom and decided to look UP know about it. Rebuilding a heart is not impossible. But it takes help and love and camaraderie and patience. Smiles can be reborn. But the self must be let go of. The heart must be given reign over the new kingdom.

There are broken hearts hiding everywhere.

Old people can be first responders if their hearts are free to see what can be.

Old people can't move around as much, but they know what you don't.

One helping hand can save a heart.

<u>S</u>ave <u>M</u>y <u>H</u>eart

<u>S</u>t. <u>M</u>atthews <u>H</u>ouse

Passionitis

I have just created a new word!

It is not in Wikipedia! Oops...

Someone else is using it...

But not in this context.

Passionitis is a passion for passion.

And I think it leads one down some questionable streets...

Where legs intertwine and the senses are celebrated and exploited.

Passion can be beautiful as long as it is honest. Where commitment means just that.

If we drop back for a moment... and look from afar... one can see passion driving so many moments both good and bad. Passion can be the fuel of creativity.

Every person that finds a passion to pursue can live outside bureaucracy. Artists survive because of passion to their brush. If you want to help a young person tell them to follow their passion... Or find one to follow. It requires humility and honesty.

I have just created a new word!

Things you don't have to pay for.

Here we go again…

A lot of old people know about passion and its pitfalls. Maybe a passion should be first to find some old coot who has been there. Someone who started a company from scratch, and was honored to provide livelihoods for his employees. This can be one of the greatest rewards of "Passionitis".

You can feel real excited and passionate about temporal passion. Like last night's… LOL

But profound passion comes from giving of yourself to those in need. It lasts and lasts and lasts. You would never brag, but the proud feeling is yours and can never be taken away.

Being passionate about the right things and doing good makes you at peace. Others will be attracted to you because you ask nothing of them.

It is better to try passionately and not succeed. Knowing you gave it your best means you don't have to look back… Just find a new passion.

We need people who are passionate about values.

Who are passionate about bringing traditions back to the classroom.

Who are passionate about not removing God from "In God We Trust".

Can you imagine the dollar bill being changed to "In Us We Trust"?

I Am Somebody

There was a book entitled "I Am Somebody."

It is no longer in print.

Can't find copies that are reasonable.

It is about a black man, Bernard Waddell, who became a Navy Frogman in the 50's. They were the precursors to today's Navy SEALs. Underwater Demolition Teams became the SEAL Teams.

This is hard training, really hard. He wrote the book about himself. You see he wanted to be somebody and did… Really did. He became one of my instructors.

Everybody wants to be somebody… all of us. Except that nobody ever defines what a somebody is. So we think celebrities are somebody. Or people who have won awards. Or sports figures. Or beautiful people. Or wealthy people.

That's the way it comes across from childhood on until we see the light. All of the above are really nobody. And many cannot live in the past and they have tragic endings.

The poorest person can be somebody. Mother Teresa became

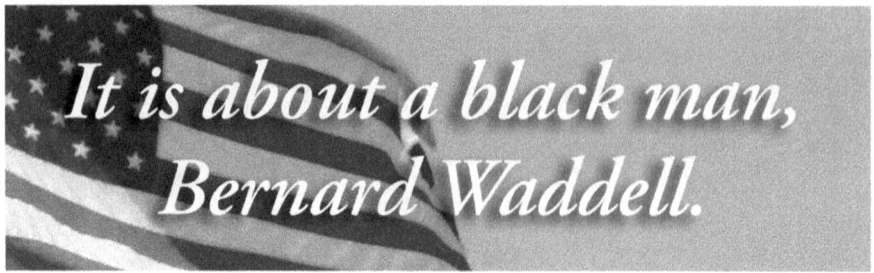

It is about a black man, Bernard Waddell.

somebody. Who wants to help the poorest of the poor all day? Like in Haiti or the Middle-East where nobodies barely survive.

Making a nobody somebody means looking someone straight in the eye and saying "I will pray for you". In that moment you become a somebody.

Or better yet… "How can I help you?" and then find a way to. Most of us are reluctant to take that first step. Until we do we are not yet a somebody.

Step back and think about the people you really admire. Not the celebrities and their causes and checks. It is the neighbor who is helping the neighborhood kids build a campsite or basketball court, while telling them about things that matter. About right and wrong. Good and evil.

Like Instructor Waddell who was teaching us how not to get killed.

He was Somebody to me.

I am Somebody.

Senior Moment

There is a time in life where your demographic status is turned upside down.

War baby, millennial, income, age, gender, over 30, under 30.... marrieds, singles....

There is a science to grouping each of us to fit into statistical boxes....

And we do not give anyone permission! Maybe one can be an appropriate exception?? Who do you call to sort things out? A demographic attorney?

Am I now a geezer, a senior, an old person???

It is easier talking to old people because they understand. Young people act like they do, but we know otherwise.

There were moments when I forgot things when I was young. Like forgetting when an explosion was going off...LOL...

Little things are harder to remember now. It doesn't matter. Except my wife is younger and reminds me of everything...

Little things are harder to remember now.

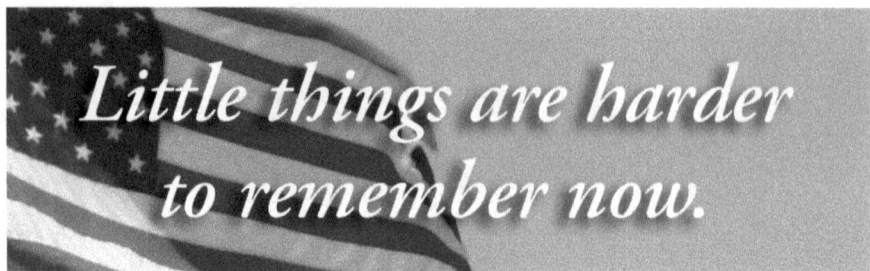

I stay busy and hopefully I won't get caught in senior moments that others can see. I don't like "senior moments". I am not a senior. I am a dynamic, honest, caring man who is ageless other than a little stooped and find it is hard to pick things up off the floor. And there are other private issues we will gloss over for now.

How about not being a senior until you are in assisted living? We have 90 year olds driving around town these days. Now that's a living senior!

I am beginning to forget what I am looking for in the supermarket or Costco or PetSmart after turning purposefully down an aisle. It's great because nobody can see you.

There is another demographic and that is "people over 10 who help others". It's an ageless demographic as age is irrelevant. As is the age of the demographic of the person helped. When the heart takes over there is no time for analysis and statistics and meetings.

Just do it.

"Just do it" is my new demographic.

I am trying to get others to sign on.

To be independent of political correctness.

To follow no rules but those coming from your heart.

What others think puts them in the "Too Bad" demographic.

Too Bad.

Hey why am I writing this??

Heart Monitor

You can put these darn things on your arm or wrist and become a digital cardiologist.

The funny thing is that more young people wear them than old people.

The fitness revolution has created products that will help us know how we are under both stress and peace.

Now you can have something to compare and gab about socially. I think you turn your monitors off when you drink and want to have fun. As long as it looks good in the morning.

I really don't know where women put them with their skinny jeans. Pockets already taken by bulging cell phones.... LOL

I won't say this is all self-centric... but think about it.

Our hearts pump oxygenated red fuel to the entire body. The heart is where it is all at even though we think it is the brain... LOL

Hearts have muscles. They have to be strong to take all the punishment we impose on them. From running miles and miles and from love. We want it to work wherever we take it.

Hearts pump fast when one is scared.

Hearts pump fast when one is scared and… in love……
hmmm..?? Check the pulse.

In a more important vein… pun… Hearts direct us to what is
good and right for us. The problem is that we mostly choose not
to listen. I don't know where else one goes in a jam for answers
when Google is not available.

Why do our hearts hold so many answers? Why does it take so
long… so many years to fully listen to it? Go talk to a person who
knows. Generally old people have finally figured it out. Eureka!

They have stories about how they didn't follow their heart and
where it led them. The time wasted. The people hurt.

Our hearts scream that others are more important than self. That
listening to it makes it easy to see needs and hurt where one can
help. How the heart got that smart is for all of us to think about.

Some say there is a form of Spirit there. It is almost like it is a
moral compass?

Heart monitor?

When you don't listen the police find you.

And give you a heart-to-heart in their patrol car on the way to jail and heart rehab....

If you are lucky they might drop you off at a Church.

Keep Clapping

What in the world are hands for?

They can pull, they can push, they can salute, they can pray, they can hit, they can hurt. There are exactly 103 other things hands can do.

Go to a movie… do they clap at the end? They clap in Giants Stadium, they clap at the Olympics. Where clapping is spontaneous it sings praise and thanks for the entertainment. They don't clap at church?

Clapping can also show genuine appreciation and respect. It can also be a form of love, of a genuine response that touches the heart.

We never really think of clapping as anything to be singled out.

But the power of clapping at just the right moment can be profound. It can turn sadness into joy. It can turn the invisible into the visible. It can wipe the tears from a child's face. "I am proud of you" touches deep inside everyone. Everyone wants to hear those words at some time if not every day. In this context clapping becomes a gift we can give others at a moment's notice.

Your clapping can change a moment.

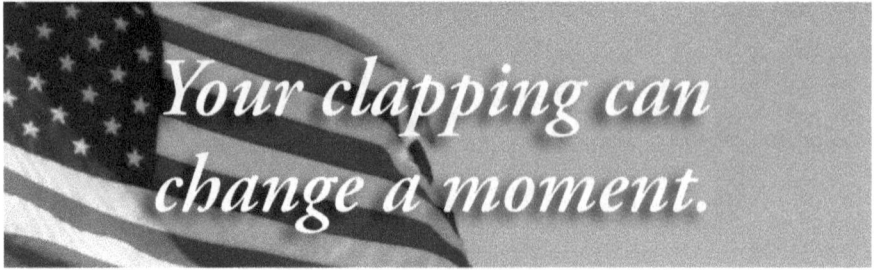

Think about it. Your clapping can change a moment. It can bring pride and reassurance in an instant. The wink or smile reveals its meaningfulness.

We all possess this tool to make a difference.

We can make a difference in someone's life with one clap.

Keep on clapping.

Stand up and clap for what is right.

That is how old people stay young.

The Painter

There are painters of houses.

There are painters of planes.

There are painters of graffiti.

There are painters of life.

There are painters of emotion... Van Gogh.

There are painters of poetry... Monet.

There are painters of people... Rembrandt.

There are painters of humor... Rockwell.

To my left in my office is a painter doing a white wall. He also paints oils of yet to be discovered passionate reality. His work takes my breath away. He has been paid pennies for masterpieces. I think he is now on the road to being discovered. I hope to be around then.

You see... He spent nine years in fear as a young man in a political prison in Cuba. Some gift was given to him somehow to survive. Emotion flows from his brushes.

There are painters of emotion... Van Gogh.

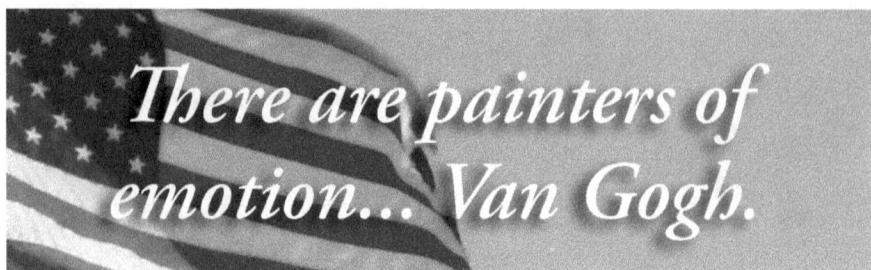

Life throws curve balls we never see coming. Our youth now hide behind the shield of a social network. Their brushes will never touch a real canvas.

Each one of us is a brush with a canvas waiting for us. Each one of us has the potential to create a masterpiece. We sell ourselves short and just paint the town, so to speak....

Our oils need to be created. They are the colors of humility and caring. When you help someone else out of a dark corner or moment you have begun a masterpiece. If you are led by your heart you will see it. If not, you blinked at your potential.

The older you get the easier it is to see your oils and where they need to go. For every soul is a canvas waiting to be loved.

Love and Truth are the brightest of pigments.

Every person's canvas screams for them.

Any person can be an immortal artist.

Don't be afraid to use the right paint.

PS: I now own a Chavez!

Room 109

109 is just a number.

Numbers mean nothing until they do.

PT 109.

Patrol Torpedo boat 109.

John F. Kennedy did some swimming in the western Pacific when it sank in WWII.

And alone from Plum Pudding Island he swam to find help for his stranded crew.

He was on the swim team at Harvard.

He became President just to be assassinated.

It hurt us.

We humans work together in all kinds of circumstances for all kinds of businesses and efforts.

If you are lucky you get to be close to the people you work with on a daily basis. First names and nicknames are traded as hybrid

I wish all us old people had a Room 109.

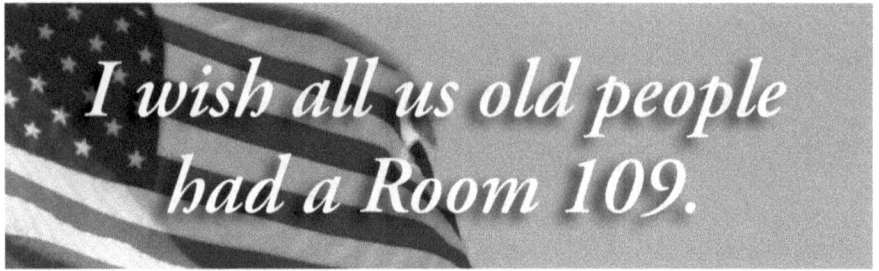

family bonds form. You look out for one another. Politics kills trust………..

Most contemporary businesses are often too structured. Efficiency and profit are elusive if all aren't working closely with trust and on the same page….

Just like a swim buddy on a 10-mile ocean swim… if you have been there…

If an executive has experienced every job in a company, his first-hand knowledge shows. A respect for all tasks is felt. It's why the best rise through the ranks.

Being close to employees can be criticized but it can also make for amazing efficiencies. As a family that cares for its family. For all to benefit from the work ethic that makes one feel that one is working for one another. Makes for a tight ship?

I retreat to my Room 109 most days to help open and mark jewelry. Thousands of items in their small plastic bags need to be opened and sorted. I have the honor to work with 3 ladies…. One from Peru, one from Cuba, and one from Mexico. We have spent many hours together hunched over… looking down at the immediate task at hand. I don't speak Spanish any better than they speak English. We are the family in Room 109 that no one sees. What we do is important. I get to see and feel what their day really is.

My back aches and I go back to my office… feeling relevant.

I wish all of us old people had a Room 109 we could go to and help out.

We may be slow, but others seeing that we care is powerful.

And it is also nice to get a pat on the back from a young person.

And we can pat them back.

109 is locked at night.

Too Old

Do not tell me I am too old.

Maybe you are too young to understand!

Wisdom is not for free.

If everything was left to young people the earth would not have survived the party.

Muscle, athleticism, and endurance works fine for marathons and enduros and football and risk. Rebounding from anything when young is doable. You can laugh at fate when young. So you think.

Don't say I am too old to drive. Here in town there are so many old people driving that you often cannot see the head above the steering wheel. Hello?? Anybody in there?? Then again, the cell phone is always lowering heads too. If you didn't look twice one would think driverless cars are already flying out of the dealers... LOL

Too old to help out? I don't think so. Been there, done that. Hey young people we know more than Google. We know what not to do. We know how to get there quicker. We have finally figured out what matters... and it is different from what you think.

Don't say I am too old to drive.

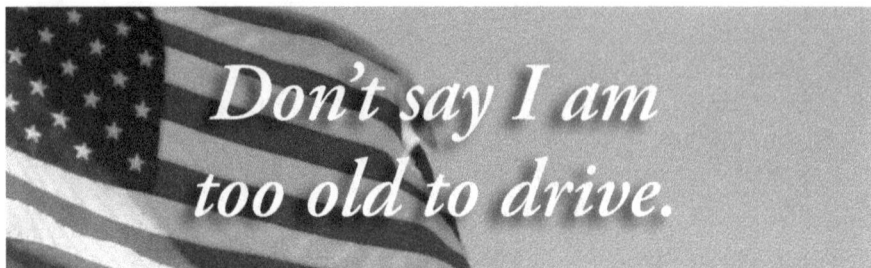

The "Too Olds" are everywhere.

Waiting to be your Eagle Scout.

Waiting to tell you what love really is.

Waiting to help you before you are too old.

Before TV

My dad was born in 1908.

He is gone.

He was good.

They still had horse drawn carriages in the streets.

The first cars were novelties.

There was no radio.

Now that is almost like science fiction, especially to a teen of today who probably mutters under his breath…"who cares"… and continues his texting.

My claim to fame is that I was born before TV.

I remember sitting on the floor at a neighbor's house. Big Dumont console with a 4" screen. I built crystal radios. We played outside for hours. Went anywhere in the neighborhood and into the woods. Came back tired from fun.

WWII ended. Victory gardens were no longer needed.

Veterans were embraced and cared for. All went back to business.

My claim to fame is that I was born before TV.

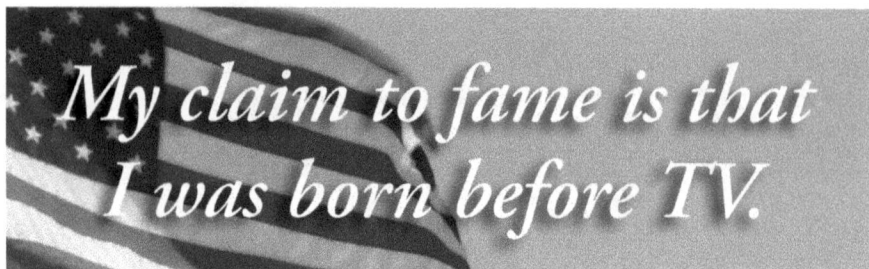

Employment was not a problem. Respect was the norm. Honesty valued. The handshake pre-empted the thousands of lawyers of today.

Then things changed. Immorality was embraced in music and culture. Free love was distorted. Love is a free gift. And genuine love is a precious miracle. But the love of drugs won.

Politics has become driven by the sensitivities to the minority and insensitivities to the majority. "Inversion politics?" Political correctness has become the cancer of tradition and what is good. Good has been redefined as bad. Values have been reduced to currency. Christianity cannot be a word in school vocabulary. It is the most criticized religion. It has been demonized and neutered. Kids are taught to be very wary of it. The tragedy of the Middle-East is just the network evening news. The abuse of women and children is less important than protecting cultural bigotry. We accuse ourselves of being the only bigots. Go figure? Inverted politics?

Heads are cut off and children bombed and we talk about global warming. SEALs go behind enemy lines and we talk about global warming. Celebrities copulate and magazine sales at checkout surge.

That is the gift to those who were born before the cell phone.

Ask any young person and they won't have a clue what we are talking about.

What about those who will be born before the End?

Let's check back on my dad's birthday again…

Stories

"Tell me some stories grandpa…"

I am still waiting for that question… LOL

There are 100 million books with stories in them. Fiction or non-fiction. The non-fiction are supposed to be true. So are history books except for the fact they are being rewritten from points of view. It seems that some facts are no longer acceptable.

We watch endless mind-numbing stories on TV. It's ok except that it tunes out your reality sensors. You are marginally less able to discern reality.

We all have our favorite stories that were told to us by a real person along the way. Especially vivid are the ones one heard as a child. Every story has a message. Sometimes the message is not good for you. You had better know the person you are listening to so you know what to think after being messaged… LOL

Some important stories to really have correct is how our country was formed. What the sacrifices are that have been made by whom along the way. Real blood shed for real reasons like love of country and love of freedom.

"Tell me some stories grandpa…"

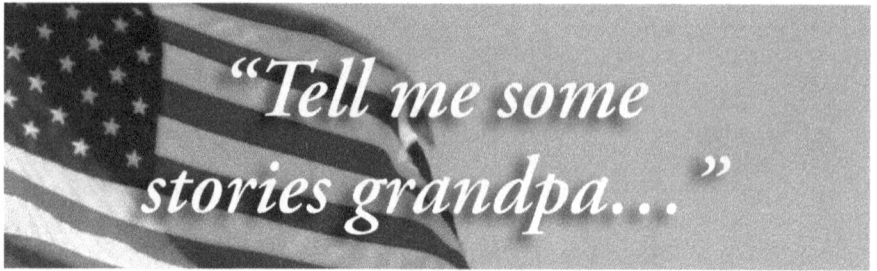

Stories of immigration. Stories of prejudice. Stories of caring. Stories of courage. Stories of love. Stories of children. Stories of family. Stories of waste. You name it we got it. Pick your network. Pick your library. Pick your Google. Pick your brains.

We have to find the stories that make us better. We need better filters these days. We need stories about good. We need stories about values. We need stories about self-sacrifice. We need stories about helping others. We need stories about humility. We need stories about respect.

It happens to be Christmas Eve and also my grandson's birthday. Kind of funny timing…?? Just happened. I have given up trying to figure out how these words get on all these pages. 11 books. Crazy. That is a story in itself.

I know where my story started.

Bethlehem.

Now that's a story.

Yes Sir

Now this is a crazy story.

One of our great gals, Vickie, was in the nail salon talking to whoever was next to her.

Her brother had been in the Secret Service...

Because I had been in Naval Special Warfare she said we should meet.

So in a few days in walks this big guy who had spent 25 years as a Secret Service agent... doing everything we can't talk about and protecting presidents. He had written a history of the Secret Service and has a fantastic spy fiction novel I am just starting.

Though I was in only for a couple of years we still had this powerful bond of serving our nation. All veterans have it. They just don't talk about it. Who would understand anyway?

I think we will become friends going forward after the holidays. I called him about something and he was at the airport on his way to family stuff in Minnesota. I said we had to get together when he got back. His response. "Yes Sir".

Her brother had been in the Secret Service...

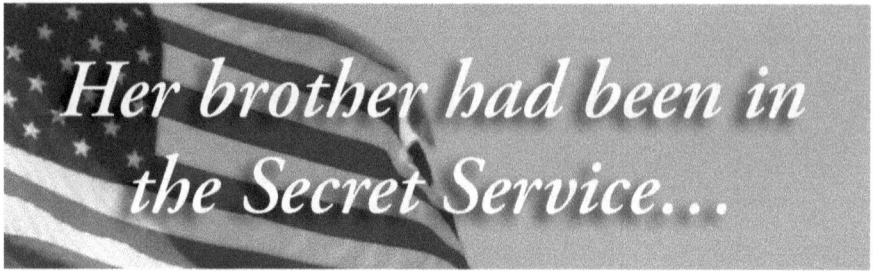

Now that makes me feel like I am an old man. Which I am. But it screams training and respect. He pretty much had to say "Yes Sir" to everyone in the White House and the 100's of people he reported to over the years.

Go in the Marine Corps and you learn the hard way how to reflex automatically ... "Sir, Yes Sir". Louder!!! "SIR, YES SIR".... While you are doing 100 pushups.

Respect is essential to making things work.

Young people today give respect no respect. They are in for a rude awakening. It will cost blood.

Why has respect been mocked? Why can't tradition be respected? Why can't manners be respected? Why is disrespect the sword of special interest and minority rampages? Law and order is an evil? Who judges whom these days? Who defines what is to be respected?

I am really sorry, but Christianity certainly should not be dis-respected. The finest people I have come across have got it all together. They figured out that values and caring was the only road without holes. We are allowing the potholes of life to distract us from our drive.

Stupidity and arrogance fuel weak egos.

It's true.

Again, I am for universal draft.

How else will the kids on our streets learn respect, and how to say "Yes Sir"?

I have learned to look up to the Heavens and say "Yes Sir"…

Hearty Meal

This food thing started as far back as I can remember. LOL.

Eat your peas Chris... my mom would say.

I remember when I pushed them under my baked potato skin and my brother told on me...

Fast forward to January 1964. Hell Week. (Google it). Eating all you could stuff down in 10 minutes then running it all off in the next 30. Don't know how the heart ever pumped so much blood. 10 hours sleep in a week. Running, swimming, obstacle course, 24 hours a day. A hearty meal took on a new meaning. Always be full as you never knew what was around the corner. Plan in advance where your next hearty meal will come from. And I don't mean fall asleep in a Burger King parking lot.

Our bodies get most of the attention in our lives. Health and fitness are culturally desired. Forever young is the promise. Body-centric becomes our new focus. Eat healthy. Whole foods make you whole. Hearty no longer means full, it means low fat, nutritious, and wonderful conversation.

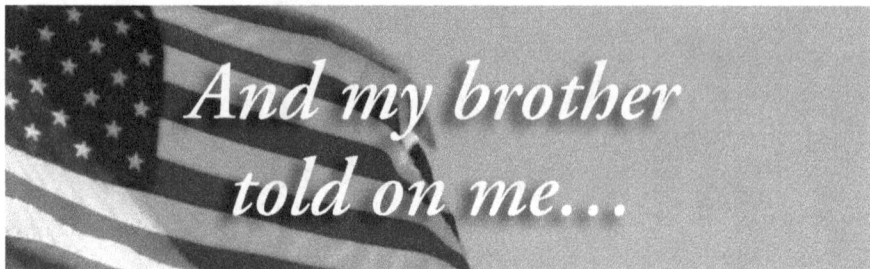

And my brother told on me…

I have had a lot of hearty meals over the years. Mine ended up with a double bypass and pacemaker. I finally figured it out.

Now that you have brought up the heart… LOL, what are we doing about it? The heart needs food too. Your heart is your sense of fairness and truth. It is where all feelings of love start. We damage our hearts often by not doing what it tells us is right. By pushing the peas under the skin. If we want our hearts to be strong then we have to let them do good. "Do good" means helping someone else. Not helping yourself… to more… LOL

Hearty meals are not found in fine restaurants but in fine humans who are willing to serve others with humility and a smile.

Boy… does your heart get to feel good.

No one else knows but you.

That is the way it should be.

Chow down.

Night Vision

If a bright light comes on keep one eye closed to preserve your night vision.

Comes in handy going to the bathroom at night... LOL

But more importantly at night all is dark.

Evil is more at home at night.

Evil doers do not like to be seen.

They do not want accountability.

That is why a lot of the things man chooses to do or celebrate is at night. It is more comfortable. Certainly, to drink...

Military and law enforcement helmets all have night vision goggle brackets on them. Osama got to see the state-of-the-art ones... briefly.

We need to know what is going on at all times of the day by all things and all people. The world is more dangerous and unpredictable than ever. And... we usually find out about it immediately. Unless it is in the media and distorted in some way. We need to see through that too.

Evil is more at home at night.

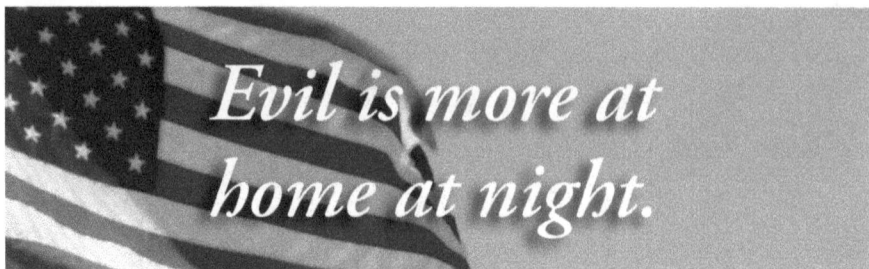

This is all really about wanting to know where evil is at all times. If we don't stay vigilant then bad things can happen that we could have thwarted or interdicted.

Don't we love our freedom, joy, peace, and love? Let's not give it away by being naive....

After dark and when we are asleep our minds are active sorting out the day's events and thoughts. We are not conscious of this until we wake up and revisit yesterday. Usually we have some new or less tired vision of what to do or think.

75% of all my chapter titles come to me in the middle of the night. I force myself to wake up and send them to my e-mail via the Captio app. I have no idea where or when they may be used.

I like 2 word ones. When they are chosen and started I go with the flow and the vision take shape in crazy ways... like now. I call it Night Vision.

You see... all these books are really meant to help us cut through the darkness.

To see what is more important than the less important.

To put a light down the right lane and to illuminate the potholes.

Night Vision Goggles on.

Stack up.

Truth Train Go!!

Best Friends

Everybody has a best friend.

You marry one.

One lies at my feet.

She's golden.

We have best friends at work.

We have best friends in our family.

We have best friends in other countries.

We have best friends in big cities.

We have best friends in small towns.

We have best friends we e-mail.

We have best friends we text.

We have best friends we take pictures of.

We have best friends in nature.

We have best friends from our pasts.

Everybody has a best friend.

We have best friends in pain.

We have best friends in trouble.

We have best friends who help others.

We have best friends in heaven.

We have best friends in our heart.

We have best friends yet to come.

Invisible

There was this TV show in the 50's in black and white... appropriately.

It was about a millionaire who quietly came across people in need. People who had experienced misfortune, who were good people at heart. He would give them 1 million dollars anonymously. The show ran for 5 years. I was moved by it. It planted a seed.

J. Beresford Tipton was the invisible man. As it should be with all of us when we do something for someone else. If one is in it for the recognition, then it isn't a gift.

It can be a dollar in a cup or $10 in a hand or a money order to another land. The more invisible one is the cooler it is. It is cool to be cool. LOL

I am not so sure how many of us actually do anonymous things. Everybody these days wants recognition. You know, an unselfish selfie. Invisibility is harder to achieve these days without camouflage and cunning.

Then there is the tip at the restaurant. Slipping a 20 into her hand

Celebrities can no longer be invisible.

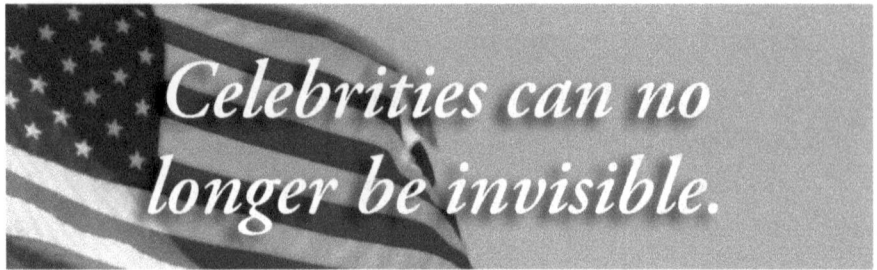

unnoticed in addition to the 20 seen on the check. No one has to know. A glance of thanks is worth its weight in gold.

Celebrities can no longer be invisible.

But we invisibles can be celebrities to ourselves if we are able to pull off the anonymous gift! Well… God knows. He will let you take an invisible bow.

There is much to do these days about secrecy. Top Secret, Eyes Only. A military trying to stay secret from enemies. Trying to be invisible so it can protect us more efficiently. SEALs live or die based upon not being seen. On not being written about.

There are many forces in life we cannot see and we are no worse for it. In these times of wanting to know everything maybe we should pause and back off.

Put our cell phone in the basket and go for a walk in the woods.

Entering a forest to become invisible and at one with nature.

Or scuba diving on a reef.

Or skiing down a mountain trail.

Or sitting on top of a hill at sunrise.

Or just looking up in the rain and feeling how unique we are.

The raindrops mingling with our tears as we find our invisibility.

Becoming One with our Prayer.

Come Fly

Frank Sinatra.

Most of our young don't have a clue who he was.

But he sure lives on.

Crazy.

"Come Fly With Me" is now being sung by Michael Buble'. It captures the dreams of escape. On a moment's notice flying to Peru, to Acapulco, to Bombay, to Heaven???

Don't we all dream of just leaving all the pain and uncertainty of responsibilities behind? And just live on a "5 O'clock Somewhere" beach?

But life is not about having fun unless you have earned it. Many have to do manual work 7 days a week in oppressive conditions. They will never get close to a real plane.

It is almost as if the devil is always whispering in your ear to take it easy. To take the easy way out. Maybe just a small lie. So you can fly.....?

The melody of "Come Fly With Me" is so seductive.

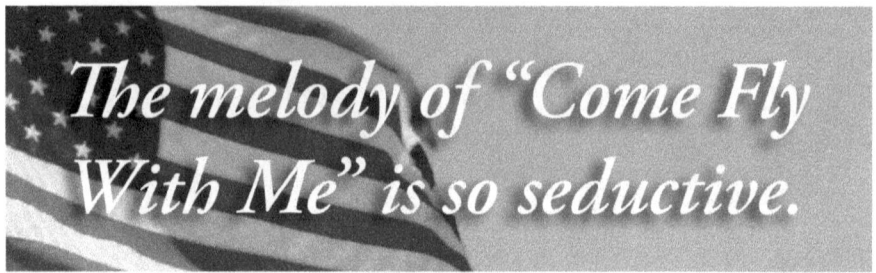

But the melody of "Come Fly With Me" is so seductive. Why not just leave everything you should be doing behind? Consequences?

If you really want to fly. If you really want to soar…. Then make your landing strip the heart of someone in need. Fly around looking at every person that you come into contact with. And see if you feel they might need some encouragement.

Land on it and don't take off until they smile.

You can wink back as you climb to look for new opportunities to make a difference.

To matter to someone.

With this in mind, maybe "Come Fly With Me" is a heavenly signal.

To let your pilot be He.

Heroin

There are no precise statistics.

Just guesses.

As to how many people use.

As to how many lives go nowhere. 100,000 do die annually from it in the USA. Think about it… 100,000 people who could have been loved and who could have loved; who could have made a difference in the lives of so many.

If you add all the other drugs… then 500,000 die annually from overdose.

It all has to do with insecurity, lack of self-worth, and tough love that came too late.

Let's play with the word "heroin". I see it as a "hero within". All the lost lives are people who wanted to be a hero but were never taught. Dysfunctional families, no mother and father, poverty, no role models nearby. Lonely girls and lost boys struggling to be adults. Their sense of self… raped by the euphoria of drugs.

There is a hero inside every human. The media makes it appear

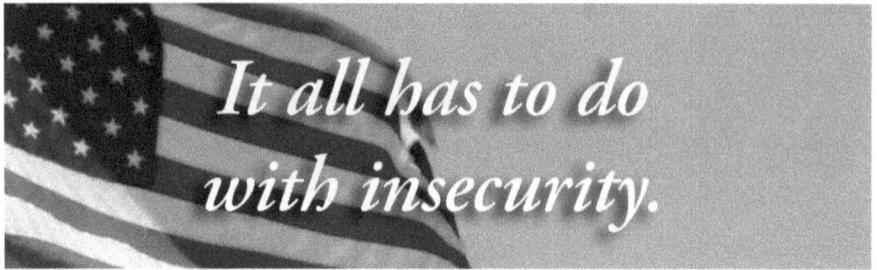

that you have to be a celebrity or fighter pilot or fireman or policeman or EMS driver even.

The real heroes are the ones who take your hand and say NO…. Who tell you what is bad is wrong as it robs you of your self.

The real hero points out what is good.

The real hero is not vain.

The real hero is never seen.

Be one.

Nobody has to know why you are smiling

Last Selfie

We spend our lives managing our self-image.

We want people to see us a certain way.

We like the right compliments.

We are often uncomfortable adjusting to our imperfections.

Along comes the cell phone and our control is in chaos. People taking pictures and texting them all over the world and we don't have control.

There is no plastic surgery... oh... maybe Photoshop ...but it's too late. Someone took an unflattering image of you and it is in Hong Kong within a minute.

Everybody loves selfies these days. Take one with Hillary, take one with Beyonce', take one with Blake, take one with a policeman..... I can envision walls of selfies in teen bedrooms.

Selfies are taken by gang members and church choirs. There are no statistics on deaths by selfie. But a serious side effect is loss of self.

To us old people our last selfies is not of much concern. Most

of us have taken few if any. We kinda never fit in with this self-centered explosion. In fact, I refuse to take a selfie. Maybe in consideration that it may be my last?? LOL

There is something about a selfie that is never flattering anyway. Chins become bigger as one holds the camera with one's extended right arm. Smiles always look a little weird too. Nope, not for me. Wrinkles play into it too.

Now, the selfie generation would probably love a TV show based on selfies. Great plots ending in great places for the ultimate selfie with 100's of worthless ones along the way. LOL

Getting serious about a last selfie? Wouldn't it be nice to take one with someone you have helped? That would tell the most about yourself.

Maybe it is better to take your last selfie when you still are young. But then again if it is to be your best effort and self-defining moment it really has to be planned out. However, when things are planned they look planned... and vain....

The last selfie must make a difference. And the only way it can make a difference goes back to helping others.

In fact, there doesn't have to be a last selfie if they all are with the people that you mattered to… that you served…

That's it.

Self service is service to another self.

Only Matters

It only matters if you do.

Nothing matters if you don't.

There are waste of time matters.

There are important matters.

If we don't figure out what matters, then we are irrelevant.

There are things which matter to our kids.

The Truth matters.

Respect matters.

Love matters.

That's all that matters.

Figure that out.

Then you grow up and matter.

Then you can see what matters.

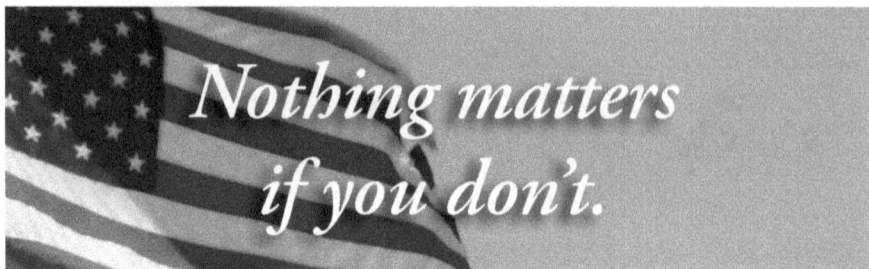

Nothing matters if you don't.

Then you can fight for what matters.

Then you can die for what matters.

He did.

Wholly Spirit

They say whole wheat bread is the best for you.

It is brown.

White bread is not good for you as it makes you fat.

I don't know…

Tell that to the French.

They say you are what you eat. Whole Foods is supposed to give you healthy foods so you don't have to worry when you walk in… supposedly. Fruit, fish, vegetables… you know… so you can be thin and beautiful and happy spirited.

Whole grain cereal. Meats free of chemicals, antibiotics, and growth hormones cost a little more. But heck, we get to be whole. Have you ever met a whole food person exercising? Close to perfection? Throw in a marathon and… you have found the whole person. It gets better if the person has a good job…even being rich! Now that is the whole package. And it ain't that hard.

Of course, if you want to be a SEAL then you have to give your whole body to some instructor who decides that your whole body

They say you are what you eat.

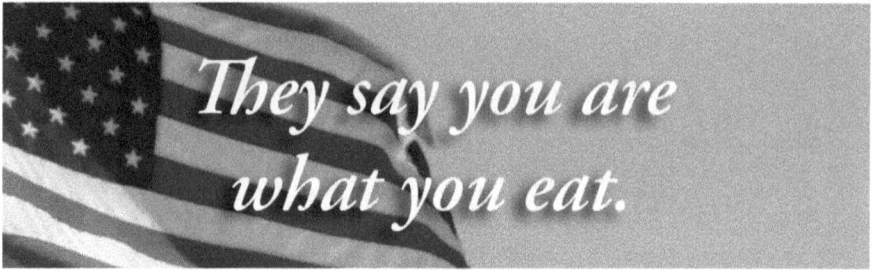

is his to do whatever he wants with it. Pretty soon your whole body is exhausted of all its wholeness and good guys begin to quit. 75% quit and decide there has to be an easier way to get whole. All branches of the military have special units where the punishing training molds new "wholes".

Oh, by the way…. You don't get to pick what you eat… or pick what you think…. Just a comment…. LOL

We try to ascend to "Whollyness" in all possible routes. Always looking for the easiest. Shortcuts to being seen as whole.

It just can't be done without giving 100% of yourself to something else. The spirit to endure must be whole. Nothing can be held back.

There are so many people out there who need help and not enough people are helping.

We can make the difference if we let go and decide we are going to matter.

We are going to give our all from our heart to others.

Some may call this a Holy Spirit.

TAPS

Tap out and the match is over in MMA, Mixed Martial Arts.

I have completed 11 books for my great grandchildren to read when they are ready.

With humor, it is all about what I think I have learned from the Navy, from family, from life, from Cursillo, and from our "No Walls" Bible Discussions in Florida and Maine.

I am not looking for a memorial service, but if one is forced on you please consider the following music: Not one song, but all.

Halleluiah

Amazing Grace

Here I am Lord (593)

Be Not Afraid

TAPS

Just the music and walk out. In church, just the music and no speeches or talks. That can happen elsewhere.

I will be watching

Just the music and walk out.

Just wink up.

I'll wink back.

You know who you are.

God Bless You

Chris

Epilogue

It has taken a little over 4 years to write these 11 books. 644 Chapters to be exact. Most being only 2 pages and driven by crazy titles out of the blue. As fun as they are, they are dead serious as I feel a war needs to be fought to rediscover the values that have made the free world so great.

Today we pander to feelings. It is destroying us.

Each chapter is a gift to the reader from my heart. Everyone will touch someone. I have already received tears of thanks from those who ventured past prejudging. Some chapters were read on deathbeds and put smiles on faces.

I know they are good. At times I felt I was just typing so fast I could not have been the writer. Draw your own conclusions.

I hammer away on converging themes… Truth. Love. Respect. Values. Serving. These are the gifts man has been given. They are gifts if not abused and ignored.

They are my gifts to you and to your families and to my family and to those who forgive me for my past mistakes.

Each chapter is a gift to the reader from my heart.

Godspeed to you all.

Chris

ACKNOWLEDGEMENTS

To all the old people I know now and to all the old people I didn't listen to before and to all the old people who made me listen. They matter.

In writing this book it became more and more clear how much family matters. Family helps shape the thinking of the young. I was blessed... most are not. Think of the Middle-East.... I never knew hunger or pain or combat. That makes one naive... and idealistic?

Old people are the veins of gold yet to be mined. The assayer would say their advice is priceless.

I have to always acknowledge those who make a difference to me. This is the short list.

There are my daughters, Candice and Courtney, who thought they knew their dad, but really didn't. There is my brilliant wife Christina, who thought she knew her husband..... And then there are my friends from the past whose life journeys I do not fully know, and who do not know me now. For in life it is who we become, not who we were.

Then there are the men of my "No Walls" Bible Studies and Max Lucado who freed us to think with assurance and humility, leading me to new friendships of the highest quality.

There are the veterans I served with and those I didn't. Ames, Riojas, Stevens, Cleary, Fry, Ross, Hawes, Hawkins, Bisset, Hernandez, Bruton, Olson, Vecchione, Phillips, Waddell and my brothers in BUD/S 31E, and countless others.... where bonding and trust was defined.

Lastly, there are Sandra Simmons-Dawson and Brian Dawson who helped edit and format the books, website, and marketing. Their firm, Money Management Solutions, Inc. dba Customer Finder Marketing http://customerfindermarketing.com/ is a gem.

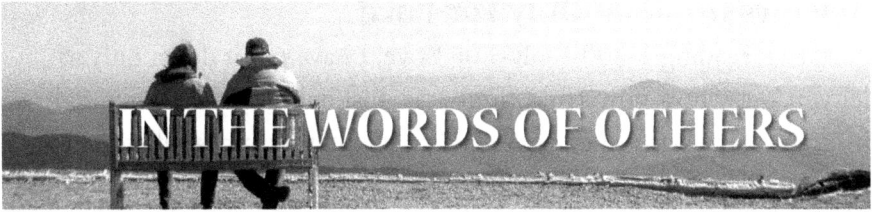

IN THE WORDS OF OTHERS

Reviews for 1-800-Oh-My-Blackness

"Chris, just got finished reading your chapters. A lot to digest, but so much of it, if not all of it, point on. I'm flattered that Nancy thinks this highly of me to offer you my opinion. What stuck out the most in the reading was values and respectability. I try to teach the young people I mentor the three "Rs", reliability, respectability, and responsibility.

Adam bomb was the bomb, I hope I'm hunched over with pride helping others."

Harold G Weeks, President, Naples NAACP

"I am a black man... better stated "am a man in black skin".

Chris, you capture and present a view of the uncolored spirit that lives inside. You have captured the unique way to challenge the heart with the eyes, the eyes with the morals, the soul with the flesh and essence of survival with eventual death if we continue to turn a blind eye to the truth that screams for change. The eyes that read this book will be forever changed. The mind will question. Long established misconceptions will be reevaluated. And hopefully change how we view, treat and learn from those born with differences."

Vernon K. Jackson

Reviews for 1-800-Only-For-Love

"I started reading 1-800-Only-For-Love. I have put it down only to let you know how powerful I think it is. Just half way through it and it brings tears to my eyes, chapter after chapter. I cannot tell you how much it mirrors my life.

We have often spoken about personal feelings and events in our lives and how similar they are. This book tells it all. What we have given up over the years in order to advance ourselves. Turning our backs on Love when really it has been what we lost, what we needed, and what we were searching for, even today.

I want to give my daughters, daughters-in-law, Ex-wife, and current roommate/girlfriend a copy to read. It says a lot that I cannot express for myself. Thanks and God Bless.

Lee Lyons – Naples, FL

Reviews for 1-800-For-Veterans-Only

"I will always have a special place in my heart for our veterans. Growing up in a military family, I spent my childhood years living on various Air Force bases, learning the lingo, and exploring the far corners of the world while my father flew various missions in both peacetime and conflict. This upbringing has given me a love and appreciation of anything written about the military, whether it be a Tom Clancy thriller or a World War II biography. Author Chris Bent has written some wonderful books in the past few years and I simply love his latest, "1-800-For-Veterans-Only".

Bent definitely has a way with words and his short essays on a variety of topics are conversational, often very witty, and sometimes quite touching. There are so many things that are touched on in this read that it would be impossible not to strike a chord with someone who has had any connection to the military over their lifetime, myself included. From thoughts on enlisting, experiences at boot camp, early days in the service and the uncertainties faced, to the battleground itself. Bent discusses not only what it's like to come home after a deployment, but the experiences of being a veteran and some of the darker aspects of this that we see in our country today.

One of the things that I found most inspiring about Bent's latest was his ability to speak directly to those veterans who may be out there and possibly struggling. There is some very sage wisdom in this one and it certainly has the potential to turn some lives around. Very well done."

TFL READER – Amazon Book Reviewer

A Veteran's Comment on the Chapter "The Hand"

"I agree because when this USMC veteran returned home there were no handshakes or high fives but plenty of shaken fists.
I'm reminded of a verse from "Where No One Stands Alone"
"Hold my hand all the way every hour every day
From here to the great unknown
Take my hand let me stand
Where no one stands alone."
There are two photos of hands representing two distinct eras:
The first is a stained glass window in a Chapel at Paris Island. S.C., with The Hand of God holding 12 Marines from my unit who were killed on Jan. 20, 1968 in Quang Tri Province, Vietnam.
The second is a marble work entitled "Hand in Hand" that stands at the entrance of a children's rehabilitation clinic in Dong Ha, Vietnam, just a few miles from the site where the above Marines were killed."

Floyd Killough, USMC (Ret.)

Reviews For 1-800-Oh-My-Donald

No matter what your politics are...

I love an interesting read that stretches my beliefs and makes me think. I have found that author Chris Bent has the ability to do just that and to entertain at the same time as I have read several of his books in the past year. His latest, "1-800-Oh-My-Donald" is a great play on Trump's run for the brass ring, but it is also much more than that. In his series of short chapters and essays, Bent gives his thoughts on The Donald but also on the state of the world, racism, evil, feminism, happiness, and even Hillary. Another well-written and most interesting read from Bent. Definitely recommend.

TLF Reader – an Amazon Top 500 Reviewer
Another blast of wit and humor

Having read almost any other book by Chris Bent ('1-800-I-AM-Unhappy' popped my cherry to the unique wit and humor Bent has been known for), I knew that at the get-go, '1-800-Oh-My-Donald' is going to be like a missile that hits you in the heart. What I love about Bent's writing is the sheer absence of pretention—Bent doesn't have any affectation, no high-brow attempts at appearing like some expert. Bent is just being himself, and he draws upon the deep well of personal experiences to write these what you may call "flash essays."

This book revolves around Donald Trump and the upcoming elections. But it would be a mistake to simply think that this book is an endorsement of Donald Trump nor is it exclusively about Trump—in fact, this book is an invitation to wonder and think about the many unspoken ponderables that strike us whenever election season comes—what is it are we really looking for, and is any of our ideas realistic or grounded in reality? What makes certain candidates tick? Why do we believe in promises? And what do we really want?

Bent's wry sense of humor and dead-pan observations pours down on you like a bucket of warm water—it is an entertaining read, like listening to the older guy hanging around at the train station. Or a kindly uncle who has been around the world and back and has a ton of things to tell you. These are pieces here that brought a tear to my eye, such as the one titled "She Works Hard." In any case, I love this book for its timeliness and for Bent's effort in collecting some of the most important morsels of wisdom from his past books. If you read the first 10 pages and you liked it, then you must realize this is also a great gift to loved ones. Highly recommended to readers of all ages!

Meghan – Amazon Reviewer, Very entertaining

I also personally find it refreshing to find an author that isn't afraid to add some humor to the current political times and situation and lighten up the mood a little bit. It seems that most people these days tend to take everything far too seriously, even much more so that the current political climate warrants. On that note, I also must say that author Chris Bent has a genuinely unique and entertaining sense of humor – it's not often that I find myself laughing out loud while reading a book, so I was quite surprised to find myself doing so several times throughout the read.

As well as this, all humor aside, the author still manages to raise some important points for discussion and debate, and he has definitely left me not only entertained, but also with a few things to ponder upon and think about more in the future. Overall, I enjoyed the read and it has given me a great first impression of the author. I highly recommend 1-800-Oh-My-Donald for any readers looking for an original and unique political commentary that I personally consider to be a more than worthwhile read.

Lucidity – Amazon Reviewer

Reviews for 1-800-For-SEALS-Only

"Pungent, cogent, wistful, idealistic, naive, wise, — all in no particular sequence, reflecting a view of life that it is all unpredictable, and it is mental, physical & moral preparation that will sustain us… there are life lessons and observations here for anyone and everyone…."

Lt (jg) James Hawes, BUDS 29E, SEAL, CIA,
(He was the First SEAL In Africa)…(sadly was my UDTR Instructor too)

"Who knew SEALs could write? (LOL) But what Chris does with his gift is really less "writing" than it is expressing the "unwritten." We all have our thoughts; and Frogmen have certain very special and unique shared experiences. Chris puts the pen to the task of relating what we (the Frogs) have experienced and what we (all of his readers) now observe in sharing the experience of the world around us. It's challenging and funny (if you've been through a "real Hell Week"), and sometimes sad. But hey, isn't life? Hooyah!"

Timothy Phillips, SEAL, BUDS 166, ST-8, ST-4

"Chris - great stuff…as always. "Hooyah Mike"…"Every sin is a grenade"…"My wife is my swim buddy"…great thoughts as only a SEAL can put into words. I love it and will BUY a few copies for my Assistant Sergeant at Arms to read to guide their young lives… Hooyah Chris and see you soon!"

Phil King, Sergeant at Arms, NC Senate, BUDS 32

"Mr. Bent's words of wisdom on some of the evolutions of U. S. Navy SEAL training are demonstrated to apply to everyday life with such simplicity. God, Family, Country, is the essence of being an honorable and patriotic American. It is the ethos of the Navy SEAL credo. The band of brothers whose lives are bonded as one in being; all for one and one for all! Nothing in this world feels better to receive in life as the emblem, the SEAL Trident, of a true warrior and to receive into one's heart the holy trinity! Hooyah! The only easy day was yesterday!"

Erasmo Elijah Riojas (Doc Rio) HMC (SEAL) Ret.

"I am a SEAL Teammate of LT. Chris Bent. During our years of serving our country as Naval Special Warfare Operatives, Chris always manifested that "Can Do" attitude so necessary for success in what many would consider: "A tough way to make a living!"

Among other sub-specialties, Chris and I had the honor of being the Platoon Commanders who would "Recover Astronauts!" Within the pages of "1-800-FOR-SEALS-ONLY", you will get to see the mind-set of students going through BUDS Training (still the toughest Military Training in the World) with most Classes experiencing an over 80% Drop Out Rate! Chris masterfully combines our training to current issues existing today. A Giant HOOYAH for a must read publication! 1-800-FOR-SEALS-ONLY is awarded a big BRAVO ZULU from your old Teammates!"

Dr. Frank Cleary, OIC, Seventh Platoon, ST-2 (Ret.)

"Five Stars for the FROGFATHER! This is a great book, and should be required reading...."

Commander (SEAL) Tom Hawkins, USN, Ret., author, NSW Historian

"Chris Bent has again taken his many and varied life experiences and applied them to life in general and "how to do it right". This book is clearly for everyone, not just SEAL's. Life was never meant to be easy and all of us can take away something from this book and the Frogman saying "The only easy day was yesterday". Even if it is the hard way....do the right thing.

From one Frogman to another I say to Chris, your eulogy (chapter 75) should be read when the time comes: Teammate, seen or unseen, you truly have made a difference!

Hooyah 1-800-For-SEALS-Only!"

Mike Macready, SEAL Team One, BUD/S 49 West Coast

"Chris Bent's latest 1-800 offering certainly gets my SEAL of approval... Using his own unique blend of insight, intellect and inspiration, Chris lifts parallels from the rich history and tradition behind the US Navy SEALs to provide challenging questions and equally thought provoking answers to this experience that we call life. In this social-networking, politically-corrected day and age where common sense, discipline and values seem to have fallen by the wayside, Chris Bent cuts through like a K-Bar to remind us all exactly what is of the utmost importance."

Darren A. Greenwell - NSW Historian, Researcher, Collector

Reviews for 1-800-Oh-My-Goodness

"With 1-800-Oh-My-Goodness, Chris Bent offers his thoughts on a variety of topics, in order to amuse, inspire, and challenge any reader. With his witty insight, and perspective forged from life experience, Chris seeks to help us all become better individuals."

Michael Hopkins, Attorney, Naples, FL

"In this book Chis is honest and open with the reader. He definitely gives you a lot to ponder. You can't wait to see what he is going to share next."

Dorothy K. Ederer O.P., Director of Campus Ministry, St. John Student Center

"Oh my goodness", Chris has again presented a faith filled and thought provoking book. His stream of thought, that often reads more like poetry than prose, will cause you to rethink moments of life in a context of love and promise."

Rev Jean Moorman Brindel, CFRE, AFP, Associate Director of
Development, Emeritus United Theological Seminary, Dayton Ohio

"Honest, incisive, poetic and profound: the writings of Chris Bent. Passion for people, the nation and the world spring from his pages; provocative questions leap from the shortest chapters ever. Silent voices speak in these pages and nothing is to be taken for granted, for life and love run deep between the lines of 1-800-Oh-My-Goodness."

Wendy J. Deichmann, PhD, President, United Theological Seminary

Reviews for 1-800-Laughing-Out-Loud

"Chis is a stew: meat, potatoes, veggies, gravy, biscuits and mustard. A warm, tender mix of good taste, generous servings, and something for all appetites! Chris mixes a Hunter S. Thompson "Gonzo Journalism" writing style with a Soupy Sales "Pie in the Face" sense of humor. Chris writes about: Life Values, Family, Self, Respect, Good & Evil. His perspective of life's Value Proposition engages our brain to think about ourselves and others. Chris' previous books are from the Heart and Soul. Take his counsel of his life's experience. There is good advice in each chapter! You will enjoy each word like every bite of a good stew."

Gerry Ross, Executive, Pratt & Whitney (Retired)

"Chris Bent is the type of guy you want to share a cold beer with at the end of a lousy day and have him philosophize on the real meaning of life. Since you might not have that opportunity anytime soon let me suggest you read 1-800-LAUGHING-OUT-LOUD. Perfect title for the book, because when reading it you will."

Nancy Lascheid, RN, BSN, Co-Founder, Neighborhood Health Clinic, Naples, Florida

Reviews for 1-800-For-Women-Only

"It is amazing that a man would want to write about women. That is a change, but Chris has a sense of humor that can make you laugh. Women will enjoy this book and men may gain new insight."

Dorothy K. Ederer, O.P., Director of Campus Ministry,
St. John Student Center, East Lansing, Michigan

"Light, refreshing take on some not so light topics. Wrapped in silliness and wit are serious, social and moral truths that challenge us to be more than ordinary."

Peggy Ryba, Membership Director, North Naples Church, Naples, Florida

"Chris is like a modern day prophet, throwing modern day concepts and concerns out there for us to contemplate. The seeds he tosses can land on sand or soil depending on the reader. I suggest you pull up a nice spot in your garden and sit down and read…then allow some of his thoughts to germinate in your life! "

Mia Guinan, Owner, Gourmet Gang, Camp Trident, Virginia Beach VA

"1-800-For-Women-Only or the "Mystery of Women" is interesting because it is brutally accurate. In fact, it is frightening to read the explanations of characteristics of women. Many of these things I had not even been aware of, but they are "right on target". The book is written with great sensitivity and insight. I never got the feeling that women were criticized, but accepted as observed. It is an easy fun read and a great gift to give to a friend or even a son who is even thinking of getting married. As the mother of three sons, I know it is true; "Heartfelt is at the core of being. Being somebody."

Sue Lester, Volunteer, Children's Coalition of Collier County,
Pilot Club, Naples, Florida

"Chris Bent's extraordinary life has given him a perspective that so very few have. His insight comes not only from his incredible experiences but from his deeply rooted sense of responsibility, caring, and love for others. His thoughtful mind is not on idle, but instead always on overdrive, crystallizing in well thought out words those concepts that would have many times escaped us, were it not for the efforts of this author to engage, care deeply, and then, as Chris has done so remarkably here, write."

Jennifer L. Whitelaw, Attorney, Whitelaw Legal Group, Naples, FL

Reviews for 1-800-I-Am-Unhappy (Volumes 1 and 2)

"This is a book by a man of many directions and passions. Straightforward yet thought provoking. Loyal to his convictions and country. And brave. Sharing. Warrior. Humanitarian."

Jeff Lytle, Editorial Page Editor, Naples Daily News

"As a friend, Chris has helped me understand the inherent conflicts embedded in the language of 'political correctness' and how it attempts, and frequently succeeds, in disguising and defeating the 'truth.' Chris is engaged in a rhetori- cal battle — we need his insight."

William Lord, a 32-year-veteran Executive Producer and Vice-President of ABC News, and Professor of Journalism at Boston University

"Chris writes like he lives. As a man of distinction, he is a voice for the poor, a champion of the truth and a friend of strong character and conviction. His word and his service are a blessing to all who encounter him."

Vann R. Ellison, President/CEO, St. Matthew's House, Inc.

"My nickname for Chris is "Dream-Catcher"- because that's who he is to me. He is my mentor in how to give on His behalf. Freely and generously, Chris offers both words, "God bless you!", and gifts. And all the while he is making a compelling and powerful statement. Chris Bent has discovered a beautiful way to live!"

Rev. Dr. Ruth Merriam, The Church on the Cape (U.M.C.), Cape Porpoise, Maine

"Chris Bent is a very unusual person – Navy SEAL, Yale graduate, successful business owner, and radical Christian who is comfortable talking with anyone at any level in society. He doesn't just talk about faith or caring about the poor, Chris actually lives his faith and he works with the poor. His smile is genuine and reflects his deep joy in life, America, hard work, people and (most definitely) God. I have enjoyed reading his writings; they are different, often hard hitting and sometimes maybe even a little wild. Each one gives a fresh perspective on contemporary lives, reflecting Chris' intel- ligence and faith. Chris enjoys moving mountains."

Rev. Dr. Ted Sauter, Senior Pastor, North Naples United Methodist Church

www.ingramcontent.com/pod-product-compliance
Lightning Source LLC
Chambersburg PA
CBHW050114280326
41933CB00010B/1101